I Love Type Series
Volume Three

Published
by Viction:ary

D1731552

Edited & Designed
by TwoPoints.Net

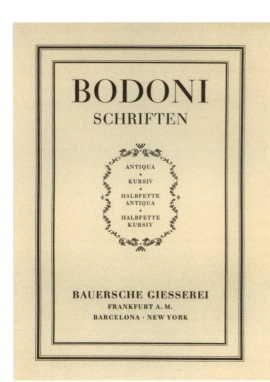

BODONI
SCHRIFTEN

ANTIQUA
·
KURSIV
·
HALBFETTE
ANTIQUA
·
HALBFETTE
KURSIV

BAUERSCHE GIESSEREI
FRANKFURT A. M.
BARCELONA · NEW YORK

Bodoni Ausgabe No.1
Bauersche Giesserei

Giambattista Bodoni created the typeface that bears his name in 1798, along with punch cuts for various sizes, used mainly for books printed in letterpress. Bodoni was an admirer of John Baskerville, and he carefully studied the designs of French type founders Pierre Simon Fournier and Firmin Didot before creating his alphabet of distinct elegance and sobriety given by the sharp contrasts between thick and thin strokes. In his Manuale Tipografico, published posthumously in 1818, there are slight differences in the shape of sizes, due to the fact that punches where handmade. Thus, the claims that certain contemporary versions are "more true to the original" are unfounded, given the variations in Bodoni's originals.

In the early twentieth century when Bodoni revival began, most re-interpretations of the typeface were based on Morris Fuller Benton's design created for American Type Founders in 1907. It is, however, the version released by Frankfurt-based type foundry, Bauersche Giesserei, in 1926, the most successful re-design, internationally known and available as "Bauer Bodoni" in digital format nowadays, due to its technical excellence and outstanding craftsmanship that characterized the Bauer foundry. Heinrich Jost, Bauer's artistic director from 1922 to 1949, was assigned to lead the job, with the difficult task of transferring the new alphabet designs onto metal punches entrusted to Louis Hoell. Hoell had gained ample experience in cutting punches at Klingspor and Flinsch, and followed Flinsch's takeover by Bauer in 1918 to work in the foundry. The resemblance to the original is clearest at a 72 point size, but the similarity is diluted as the font size decreases. With its 13 different fonts (including "expert fonts"), the Bauer Bodoni offers the most complete digital

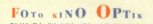

version of the Bodoni typeface. Before the digital era, the Bauer Bodoni never achieved any major commercial success in Europe, particularly because its fine serifs easily broke during letterpress printing; so printers used versions they considered more resistant. However, American graphic designers preferred the Bauer Bodoni over other versions. The problem with the serifs breaking did no occur in America, since the texts were in "layout studios" dedicated to running proofs in machines that did exert little continued pressure on the types. These layout proofs were then used for offset printing. Curiously enough, it was precisely in the U.S., where the first contemporary version of the typeface was created by ATF, that the Bauer Bodoni had its greatest acceptance.

In 1984, Swiss designer Karl Gerstner was asked to adapt IBM's visual identity in order to make it more suitable for the European market. Gerstner chose Bodoni Old Face, the Bodoni typeface adapted for phototypesetting by Berthold AG Berlin's artistic director, Gerhart Günter Lange. Berthold was also the supplier of Akzidenz Grotesk, a typography that was extremely popular in Switzerland before the advent of Helvetica. More recently, URW++ would create three digital Bodoni fonts exclusively for IBM: light, light italic, and medium.

ABC
DEFGHIJKLMNOPQR
STUVWXYZ* bauersche
gießerei abcdefghijklm
nopqrstu frankfurt vwx
yz am äöüchckfffiflß&§
fette bodoni-antiqua   .,-:;!?'(main 1234567890

Die in dieser Probe vorgeführte Schrift ist gesetzlich geschützt.
Jede Nachbildung zum Zwecke der Vervielfältigung ist verboten,
ebenso jede sonstige Benutzung, die im Widerspruch zu unseren
allgemeinen Lieferungsbedingungen steht.

Another notable version is the one designed by Sumner Stone for the International Typeface Corporation (ITC) in 1994. The version was presented in the city of Parma to commemorate the 250th anniversary Giambattista's birth on the occasion of the International Typographic Association's Annual Conference (ATypI). When ITC was absorbed by Monotype Imaging, this version of Bodoni became part of the Monotype and Linotype font library.

Originally created for setting text in books, Bodoni has become an essential visual communication component for a number corporations in different sectors, including fashion (Giorgio Armani, Helena Rubinstein), tourism (Hilton Hotels), entertainment (the musical Mamma Mia!) or, as was mentioned previously, technology (IBM). At the same time, it is reassuring to see that Bodoni is still used in books and magazines, primarily those that deal with themes related to art, including architecture, music, painting and fashion. Bodoni is, without a doubt, synonymous with creation and artistic sensibility.

Wolfgang Hartmann
Bauer Types

Cobblers	Sekt	Whiskies
Champagner, Sherry, Cointreau, Port, Cordial Médoc, Side Car, Rocardy, Grapefruit	Mumm, Deinhard, Söhnlein, Matheus Müller, Kupferberg, Henkell, Burgeff	Black & White, John Haigh, Canadian Club, Old Overholt, Johnnie Walker, American Rye
3,50	2,50	2,50

Cocktails	Special-Drinks	Apéritifs
Martini 3,–	Prairie Oyster 2,50	Cinzano 1,50
Manhattan 3,50	Nikolaschka 2,–	Port, Sherry 2,–
Alexander 3,50	Tom Collins 3,50	St. Raphael Quinquina 2,50
Bronx 3,50	John Collins 4,–	Amer Picon 3,–
Blondes Gift 3,50	Orange-Blossom 3,–	Pernod 45 3,50

Cocktails	Liqueurs	Sours
Champagner 3,75	Curaçao, Apricot Brandy 1,20	Gin 3,50
Prince of Wales 4,–	Cherry Marie Brizard 1,50	Whisky 4,–
Rauhreif 3,75	Bénédictine D.O.M. 2,50	Brandy 3,50
Fortuna Spezial 3,75	Chartreuse 2,50	Rum 2,50

Flips	Cognacs	Fizzes
Zitrone, Orange, Port, Sherry, Mocca, Champagner, Sport, Egg-Nogg, Omnibus, Butterfly	Bisquit-Dubouché, Rémy Martin, Otard G.d.E., Meukow, Roi de Rome, Hennessy, Martell	Gin, Brandy, Orange, Silver, Golden, Royal, Whisky
3,50	2,50	3,50

Elegidos
Catalogue

Tea party

Pollera, vestite y andate, for

instalacion by Puloverchito

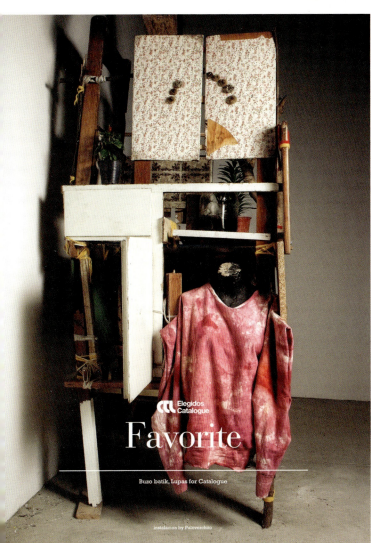

Favorite

Buzo batik, Lupas for Catalogue

instalacion by Paloverchito

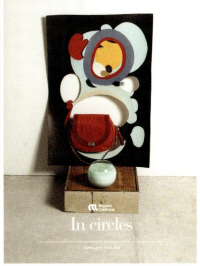

In circles

Naturaleza Muerta / / / Still Life
2010 – Installation, Sculpture and
Artwork Development
Client/Photography Catalogue Magazine
Design Hernán Paganini and Catalogue Magazine

Fashion like a Non Place.

Flower girl

Vestido, Complot, $189

Elegidos
Catalogue

Nut-brown

Buzo, A.Y. Not Dead, $189

*"The light and rigid
feel of Bodoni makes
a perfect fit with the
photography."*

Elegidos
Catalogue

Being a star

Zapatos, Natacha, $360

arte by Puloverchito

Play
with me

A MIDWINTER NIGHT'S DREAM

Photography by SHAMILA
—

Styling by Natalia Witschke (Nina Klein); Hair by Edwin Kaufmann (Nina Klein);
Make Up by Yvonne Nusdorfer (Angelique Hoorn); Photographic assistance by Peter Meijer;
Model: Irene (Paprazzi Models)

NEUE MODE MAGAZINE 7 FALL/WINTER 2006   13

Neue Mode 7   Typeface in Use
2007   Bodoni LT Bold

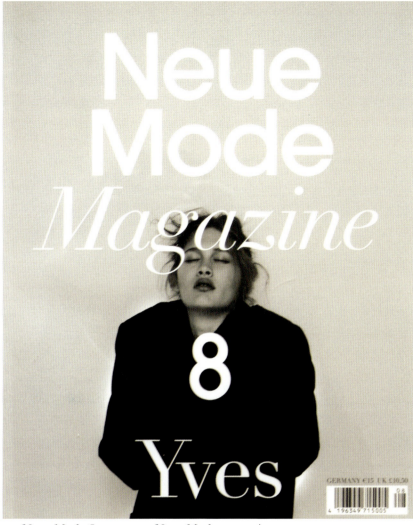

"The beautiful elegance and the ordinary beauty"

Neue Mode 8
2008

Neue Mode magazine
2006-2008 Editorial Design
Client Neue Mode magazine
Design Oliver Daxenbichler

Editorial design for Neue Mode magazine. The magazine's sense is created through the selection of unique images and its distinctive, yet simple layout. The design combines creativity with an uncompromising artistic approach, which aims at post-modernness and straightforwardness.

Typeface in Use
Customized Bodoni LT Bold,
Futura LT ExtraBold,
ITC Avant Garde Gothic LT Medium

THORN MY FLESH

Photography by BONG-KIL.

—

Styling by Christof Peat (Nina Klein); Make Up by Tom Ludwig (Liga Nord);
Models: Annelyse Schoenberger (Modelwerk), Friedrich

Skirt by BRAHM A SOSERA

Womb Asylum

Photography by Dean SAMESHIMA

—

asunne vivid astro focus; Marty and Milena portrait, 2004,
Los Super Elegantes at asunne vivid astro focus XI

Shirt by OUR LEGACY – jacket by DRIES VAN NOTEN

THE TIMES THEY ARE A CHANGIN'

Photography by Emma ANDREA

Styling by Christine Gustafsson, Hair & Make Up by Emma Lundgren,
Photographic assistance by Fredrik Ferreire, Styling assistance by Emma Lundgren,
Models: Johannes (Stockholmsgruppen), hair etc.
Special Thanks to Victoria Arena, Ragtime & music a mattis studio

Neue Mode 7
2007

Typeface in Use
Bodoni LT Bold

Oliver Daxenbichler's
Favorite Bodoni Letter
is "A".

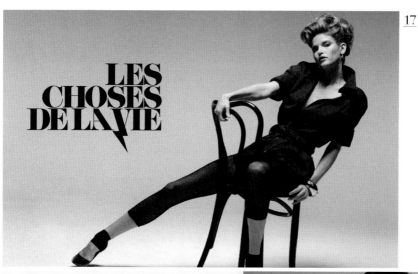

LES CHOSES DE LA VIE

JE NE SAIS QUOI!

"Its outstanding elegance"

Neue Mode 6
2006

Typeface in Use
Customized Bodoni
LT Bold

Rob Schellenberg &
Derek Hunt's Favorite
Bodoni Letter is "M".

27th Annual Fashion Show
2009 – Fashion Show Brochure
Client Iowa State Textiles and
Clothing Program
Art Direction Rob Schellenberg
Design Derek Hunt

Publication design and art direction for "The Fashion Show," one of largest student-run fashion shows in the United States. The strong modern serif was used in contrast to the show's bold san serif identity, revealing a contemporary and sophisticated composition. By modifying the type and allowing the modern serifs to bleed off the page, it gave the type an illustrative quality that often works more as artwork.

"The typefaces chosen communicated a classical and sophisticated look for the Iowa State Fashion Show. The playful use of the serifs helped build an interesting typographic construction throughout the different headlines of the publication."

2010 – Catalog
Client Kilsgaard Eyewear
Design Designunit (Jesper Johansen)
Photography Dennis Stenild

Catalog design for the award winning
Kilsgaard Eyewear

Typeface in Use   *"Beautiful elegance,*
Bodoni,   *clean and luxurious"*
Gotham

"Sahara Bodoni is 'an ultra heavy redesigned Bodoni look, extremely powerful, yet very elegant'. This summarises it perfectly. We found the typeface fits the tone of voice we wanted to achieve with our magazine."

Tom Pollard's Favorite Bodoni Letter is "g".

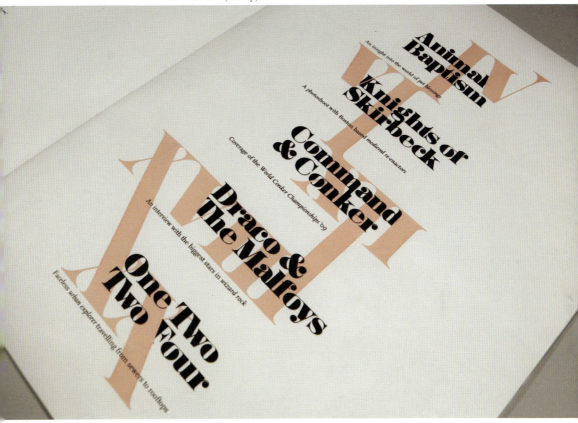

Salmon Magazine
2009-2010 – Magazine
Design Nick Dady, Paul Moffatt, Tom Pollard,
Ryan Van Kesteren

Salmon magazine is a publication with a target audience
of people interested in alternative culture. The bold typography is isolated to a salmon pink inlay, which is designed
to enhance the strong photo-journalistic style of the magazine. The defining sentence of Salmon is "swimming
against the mainstream".

GlobalFunk
2010 – Poster
Client GlobalFunk
Design Designunit (Jesper Johansen)

A0 catalog-poster for Danish jeans, GlobalFunk's Fall/Winter 2010 collection.

Typeface in Use
Bodoni

Stiletto Nyc's Favorite
Bodoni Letter is "j".

Typeface in Use
Bauer Bodoni

*"General impression,
blockyness and
elegance."*

Verrier Identity
2008-2010 – Corporate Identity, Invitation, Lookbook and
Special Book Project (Cdfa Magazine)
Client Verrier, New York
Design Stiletto nyc

The goal was to give Verrier a bold, elegant and recognizable
identity. Verrier's clothes are feminine and full of details.
Bodoni and the way we are playing with the type throughout
Verrier's identity is our graphic translation of the clothing...
The brief was initially very open just actually not to change
the logo - which of course we had to play with.

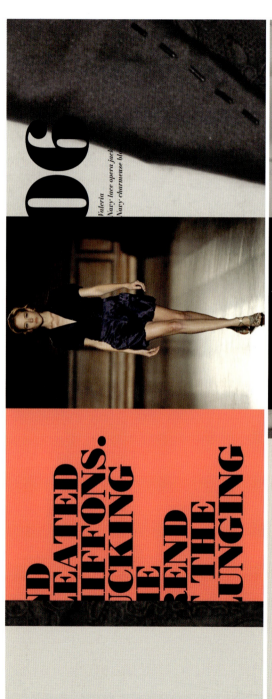

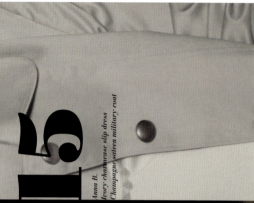

06 *Valeria*
Navy lace opera jack
Navy charmeuse ble

15 *Anna B.*
Ivory charmeuse slip dress
Champagne satteen military coat

AC
TH
NE
MA
AN
CA
PE
IN

19

Maren
Ivory satin camisole
Ivory linen academic blazer
Metallic tweed pencil skirt

28

Shu-Pei
Lavande charmeuse slip dress w/ Swarovski crystals

"According to the historical period of the late 60s we choose this typeface (Bodoni Poster), which is related to the books content."

PERFORMING 68/89

PERFORMING 68/89

Project 68/89, Performing 68/89
2009 – Book Journal
Client ZZF Potsdam
(Zentrum für Zeithistorische Forschung)
Design formdusche (Svenja von Döhlen, Tim
Finke, Timo Hummel, Steffen Wierer)

The book/journal "performing 68/69" addresses
pop culture and its liberalizing influence on
West and East European societies.
It deals with the fate of the blossoming culture
in Czechoslovakia after the violent end of the
Prague Spring. What would become of the West
and East European relationship during the nor-
malization period?

formdusches' Favorite
Bodoni Letter is "A".

Typeface in Use
Bodoni Poster (headline),
Proforma (body),
Mexcelent 3D (graphics)

Design Walk 2010, Poles Apart
2009 – Event Identity
Client Design Walk
Design G Design Studio (Mihalis Georgiou,
Alexandros Gavrilakis, Diamantis Arabatzis)
Collaborators Double Decker (Wilhelm Fin-
ger, Melita Skamnaki)

For the 2010 Design Walk, London-based curating agency, Double Decker, challenged 13 graphic design studios to create a piece of work with inspirations from contradictions and oppositions, the fundamental situations in design methodology which designers often face, in the historical center of Athens (Psyrri). The resulting exhibition, Poles Apart, gave a unique visual insight into the creative process – as well as its curious contradictions.

The visual identity of Design Walk 2010 we designed followed the conflict between "functional" and "decorative". All the applications are double-sided. The functional side is presented by two very classic and practical types, Bodoni and Helvetica. On the other hand, we used the same structure and type style on a vintage wallpaper we found in Psyrri and sprayed the paper from top to bottom, a bold and extravagant element to contrast the types. Graffiti is a key visual element of the area as well.

*"Bodoni illustrates
our passion on serif
fonts."*

G Design Studio's
Favorite Bodoni
Letter is "g".

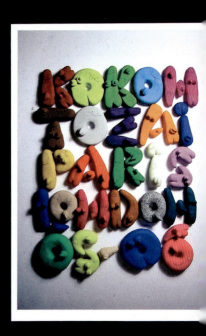

KOKON TO ZAI

JODIE HARSH & ALEX CARLÉ DJ SETS BY
INVITE YOU TO JERRY BOUTH
THE KOKON TO ZAI MED DAMON
LONDON FASHION WEEK PARTY ROKK
  ZAMIR
MONDAY 17TH SEPTEMBER ALEX CARLÉ
AT PAPER JODIE HARSH
68 REGENT STREET
LONDON W1B 5EL LIVE PERFORM

8-3AM PLEASE RSVP AT
  RSVP.KOKONTOZA
  WWW.KOKONTOZA
  WWW.JODIEHARS

Typeface in Use
Bauer Bodoni,
Bauer Bodoni Italic,
Bauer Bodoni Bold

*"Bodoni came to adequate contrast
to the rotund naiveté of the front
playdoh illustration."*

<u>37</u>

Kokon To Zai Store Card
2007 – Store Card
Client ArtProjx
Design Eat Sleep Work / Play
Illustration Yoshikazu Yamagata

This was one of the very first things we
designed back in 2007 for Kokon To Zai,
an edgy record and boutique in London.
We decided to have fun with the rainbowy
typesetting and use it to display the different designers they carried.

Eat Sleep Work / Play's
Favorite Bodoni
Letter is "G".

G

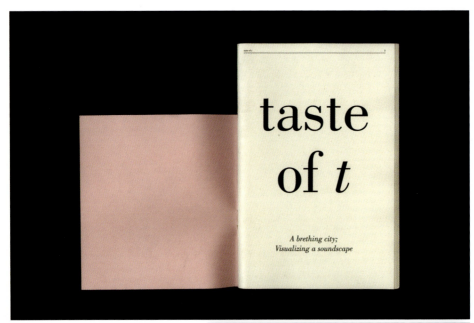

"Bodoni evokes credibility because of its thick and thin shapes and history, which fits for research projects."

g

Hoon Kim's Favorite
Bodoni Letter is "g".

Taste of T
2007 – Research Book
Design Why Not Smile
(Hoon Kim)

"Taste of T" is a research book of personal inspirations for sound visualization in the public space. It consists of various '3-Q&A' in relation to the topic, such as 3 huge objects, 3 tiny objects, 3 physical qualities, 3 abstract qualities, 3 places, 3 book titles, 3 events from history, 3 supermarket items, 3 people, 3 companies, and 3 websites.

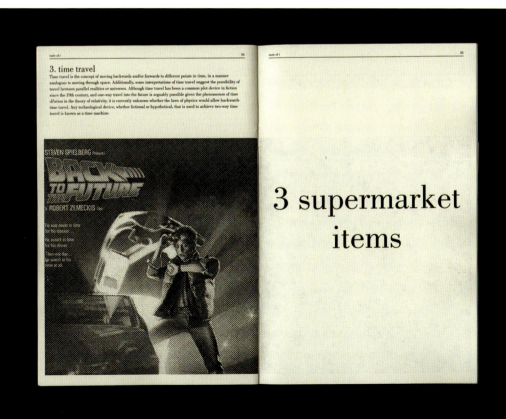

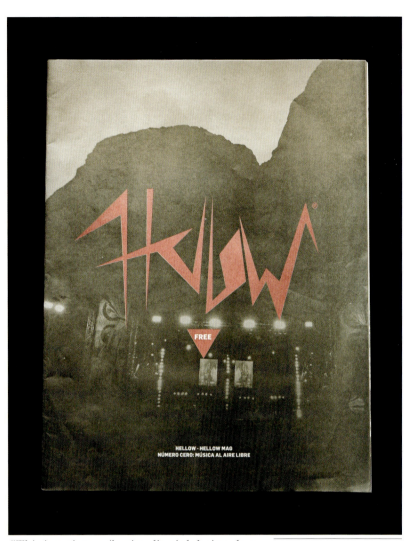

"This is a vintage/basic editorial design, but at the same time we experimented with the change of rhythms and contrast of this type-face (Bodoni Poster)."

9

Manifiesto Futura's
Favorite Bodoni
Number is "9".

Hellow Magazine
2009 – Music Magazine
Client Hellow™
Design Manifiesto Futura

The budget for production was minimal, so we
took inspiration from 1970s punk music fan-
zines. We made prints on papel revolución with
2 inks, including a fluorescent pink to compose
a modern, flashy look.

Parkdean 10
2009 – Book
Client Parkdean Holiday
Design Founded

Parkdean 10 is published to celebrate
Parkdean Holiday's ten years of successful
business, a trajectory of illustrious growth.
The book was produced as a keepsake for
the many who have been involved along
the way.

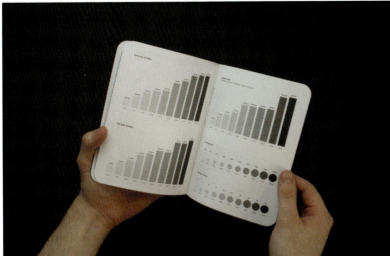

Typeface in Use
Bodoni Poster,
Gotham Book,
Gotham Book Italic

"Bodoni has a gorgeous heavyweight confi-
dence to it and the contrast between the thicks
and thins is beautiful. It has balance when
used at large sizes and always evokes the
tactile quality of freshly printed literature.
It looks great in black and white too."

"We used Bodoni to give the brochure an administration style. We didn't want to copy the actual administrative style, but to refer to the old French administration document because we love this distinguished heritage. We chose Bodoni because of its precursor drawing which is very geometrical and also because of its generous shapes. It gives the brochure a very authoritarian and precious style, which was interesting in order to speak about the paperless."

05 lettres

au Ministère de l'immigration, de l'intégration, de l'identité nationale et du développement solidaire

5 letters to the French Immigration Ministry
2008 – Brochure
Client Réseau Education Sans Frontière
Design Müesli

05 letters is published to bring the French Immigration Ministry's awareness to the undocumented facts about the illegal immigrant population in France. We decided to draw on the types to develop an administration-style brochure.

Typeface in Use
Bodoni Poster,
Bauer Bodoni Roman
Old Style (figures),
Bauer Bodoni Old
Style Bold (figures)

A Monsieur Brice Hortefeux
Ministre de l'immigration
et de l'identité nationale

Ministère de l'immigration
101 rue de Grenelle
75 323 Paris Cedex 07

01

Marseille, le 28 décembre 2007

Monsieur le Ministre,

(…) Je vis à Marseille, travaille dans une école publique qui accueille sans distinction les enfants d'un quartier populaire de la ville. Lorsque Monsieur Sarkozy, alors Ministre de l'Intérieur nous a gratifiés en 2006 d'une circulaire ouvrant la possibilité aux préfets de régulariser des familles dites « sans papiers » répondant aux critères que vous savez, j'ai découvert que des familles parfaitement intégrées que je connaissais depuis des années, dont j'avais accompagné la scolarité de plusieurs enfants, étaient en situation irrégulière.

(…) Je vais vous parler de Nejla* qui a sept ans seulement et fréquente un CE1 de mon école. Nejla est asthmatique et son père et sa mère ont quitté l'Algérie en 2001 quand elle n'avait pas un an. Ils l'ont fait pour elle, pour qu'elle ait une vie meilleure. En Algérie, la vie était devenue très difficile et ils n'avaient pas les moyens de la faire soigner correctement. Qu'auriez-vous fait à leur place, Monsieur le Ministre ?

Comme vous vous en doutez, leur demande d'admission au séjour a échoué, l'Algérie étant comme chacun sait un pays sûr et disposant de structures de soins corrects… pour les gens riches et protégés. N'étant ni l'un ni l'autre, ils sont restés ici.

« Déboutés » de la « circulaire Sarkozy », ils ont senti l'étau se resserrer sur leur fragile situation et, en plus de la honte, du sentiment d'humiliation, de la condition de parias de seconde zone, sont venues la peur, l'angoisse et la dépression (sans les soins de Médecins du Monde, le papa aurait peut-être mis fin à ses jours). Leur situation de « sans papiers » étant maintenant comme, ils sont particulièrement exposés !

Et quand vous osez dire à un journaliste qu'il y a encore beaucoup de travail à faire pour que la France ne compte plus que des citoyens propres et honnêtes, en sous-entendant que ces personnes ne sont ni l'un ni l'autre, il ne faut pas s'étonner qu'une de leur voisine, délatrice zélée de ces « mauvais » citoyens, leur ait envoyé la police à domicile. Ils ont alors dû se cacher et changer d'adresse…

Nejla qui ne s'exprime presque pas dit tout cela avec ses yeux et souvent, trop souvent, avec ses crises d'asthme de plus en plus violentes. Elle a dû être plusieurs fois hospitalisée en urgence cette année. L'autre jour, sa maman m'a demandée de prévenir le maître de Nejla. Sa fille avait passé une fort mauvaise nuit mais avait tenu à venir tout de même à l'école, son havre de paix. La maman craignait une nouvelle crise et souhaitait qu'on porte une attention particulière à l'enfant ce jour-là.

Je suis allée aussitôt frapper à la porte de la classe pour prévenir discrètement l'enseignant. En lui parlant à voix basse mon regard s'est porté machinalement sur Nejla dont nous parlions et qui nous regardait avidement. Quand nos regards se sont croisés son angoisse a explosé : elle a vomi comme jamais je n'avais vu un enfant vomir, en un jet violent et terrible. Elle a vomi de peur, Monsieur le Ministre. Elle avait cru que je venais « annoncer une mauvaise nouvelle ».

Depuis, Monsieur le Ministre, je n'ai plus de repos et je voudrais que vous n'en ayez plus, que plus un des ordinateurs et des exécutants de votre « politique du chiffre » n'en ait !

Tant que des êtres humains, dont le seul crime est de vivre sur une terre où le droit de circuler est acquis aux marchandises mais pas aux Hommes, seront menacés comme des malfrats d'emprisonnement et de bannissement, nous ne devons plus avoir de repos.

Pour Nejla et pour tous les autres, ceux qui vivent cachés, ceux qui dorment ce soir dans les prisons que vous nommez pudiquement « centres de rétentions » (y feriez-vous dormir votre femme, vos enfants, Monsieur le Ministre ?), pour ceux qui nous quittent menottés, brisés dans leur dignité et leur espoir d'avenir, nous ne pouvons plus avoir de repos !

Je ne vous souhaite pas de joyeuses fêtes, Monsieur le Ministre.

Madame Lefort

*J'aurai aimé avoir assez confiance pour parler de cette enfant en lui laissant son vrai prénom !

"Bodoni's contrast-ing stroke weights worked well to create the custom ligature."

Typeface in Use
Bodoni Book Roman

Ayr Custom Cabinetry Logo
2009 – Corporate Logo
Client Ayr Custom Cabinetry
Design Neil Wengerd

An identity overhaul produced for high-end bespoke cabinetry maker, Ayr Custom Cabi-netry.

Studio Blanco's
Favorite Bodoni Glyph
is "*".

Typeface in Use
Bauer Bodoni

L'arte contemporanea
incontra la donna
2008 – Catalog
Client Christie's
Design Studio Blanco

Cover and editorial
design for the auc-
tion catalog booklet
"L'arte contemporanea
incontra la donna" to
be published by Chris-
tie's, with Elisabetta
Farina's artwork.

"The book showcased
some artworks done
by an Italian painter.
We thought it was
appropriate to use
a straight Italian
typeface. The Bauer
variation was chosen
because of its delicate
and graceful interpre-
tation."

NotJones Design's
Favorite Bodoni
Letter is "g".

*"Beautiful curvaceous, feminine
yet 'serious' letterforms"*

Rebrand
2008 – Corporate Identity
Client Ceidiog
Design NotJones Design
Photography Warren Orchard

A rebranding project for Ceidiog, a Cardiff-
based production company. Project items
include logo applications on corporate business card, stationery and mailers.

Typeface in Use
Sahara Bodoni, Helvetica light

Typeface in Use
ITC Bodoni Seventy-two,
Filosofia Sansa

The project was to realize a series of designs to promote the prizes that Women Together presents every year in New York. This commission included an invitation to announce the winners and two brochures to distribute in the ceremony. Every item was printed on a square of stock to be handled and stored easily, and at the same time forming a unit itself. The design was done in two colors, red as the color representative of the association and black to achieve a good contrast.

Romualdo Faura's Favorite Bodoni Letter is "A".

"I was searching for a typography with personality, elegance and subtleness, which was adapting nicely to a composition with geometric elements and was combining with other typefaces I used. In this case, Bodoni acts as the leading character, around which the side actors and extras are placed, respecting always its leading roll. The high contrast in the shape and height of this typography makes it perfect for this work."

R&R Design
2009 – Corporate Identity, Direct Mail
Design Ramon Lenherr, Rosario Florio

It is a direct mail for new customers.

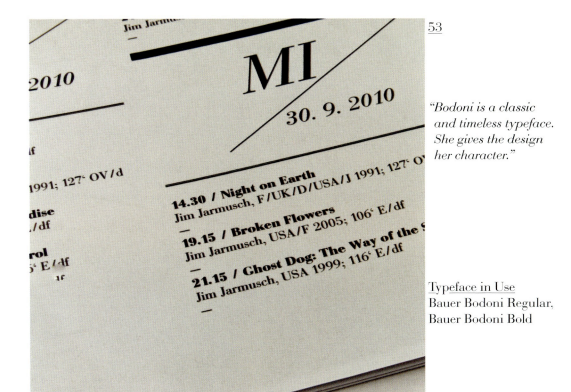

"Bodoni is a classic and timeless typeface. She gives the design her character."

<u>Typeface in Use</u>
Bauer Bodoni Regular,
Bauer Bodoni Bold

"We chose Bauer Bodoni for its classical elegance that goes well with the academical atmosphere that we were searching."

Typeface in Use
Bauer Bodoni,
Helvetica Neue

J

Exercices d'Architecture / Architecture en Exercice
2006 – Poster, Flyers
Client Institut supérieur d'Architecture Saint-Luc Liège
Design Manuela Dechamps Otamendi

Poster and flyers for the communication of an architecture festival in Liège (Belgium) presenting a series of lectures of architects as a professional practice as well as a teaching practice.

saison :

2006-07

Institut Supérieur d'architecture Saint-Luc de Wallonie

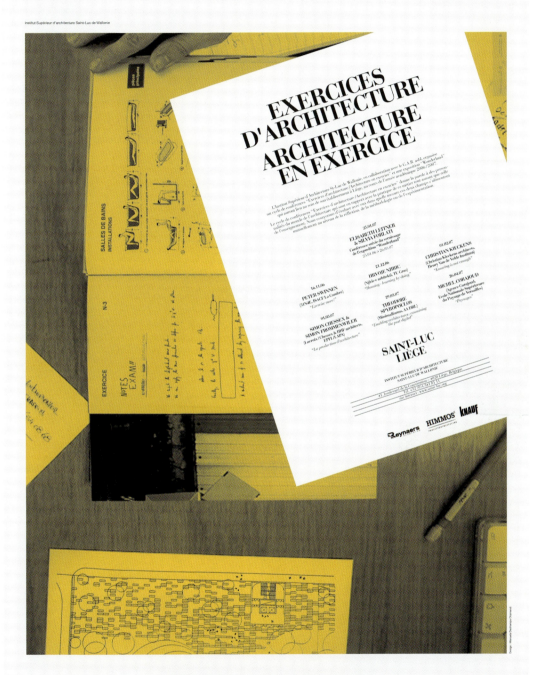

rencontres d'architecture

"(Bodoni) a classic and distinct typeface"

Typeface in Use
Bauer Bodoni

j

MusaWorkLab's
Favorite Bodoni Letter
is "j".

Fête D'Or
2008 – Invitation
Client Moet&Chandon
Design MusaWorkLab

Moet&Chandon Gold party in
Oporto city was a party by the Gold concept. Serralves museum was
the place, a very distinct art museum. Within this gold and art concept
Musa try to concept the invitation using a different size and approach.

THE BAG SHOW

28/02-02/03
2008

93° MIPEL - MILANO - RHO

FASHION TREND ZONE
HALL 16 - BOOTH A09 - B10

THE NEW HQ
Via dell 'Artigianato, 6 - 41030 Bastiglia (MO) - Italy
Tel. +39 059 815282 * Fax +39 059 816014 * info@reginabags.com

REGINABAGS.COM

Studio Blanco's
Favorite Bodoni Letter
is "!"

Spring Summer 2008 Promotional Materials
2008 – Direct Mail
Client Regina
Design Studio Blanco

Art direction and design of some promotional
card for Regina. The cards have been used to
invite clients and buyers to Mipel Milan trade-
show.

*"The brand-client has
a strong Italian herit-
age tradition, plus an
elegance, playful and
feminine attitude.
We thought it was
appropriate to choose
a font with the same
features."*

Typeface in Use
Bodoni Poster,
ITC Avant Garde
Extra Light

Packaging for Catherine Hammerton
2007 – Packaging Design
Client Catherine Hammerton
Design Studio Ten and a Half
(Charlie Bolton, Jessie Earle)

Catherine Hammerton produces bespoke wallpaper designs. A print was designed within this packaging solution which can be folded in different ways for the various products. The typography reflects the steps and pattern involved in hanging wallpaper. The subtle tonal color was used to simulate the tonal prints on Hammerton's wallpaper design.

Photography Sussie Ahlburg, London.

Photography Sam Robinson, London.

2

Studio Ten and a Half's Favorite Bodoni Number is "2".

"Bodoni and Avant Garde were used to reflect simple and elegant aesthetic of the wallpaper. In addition, Avant Garde extra light was chosen to echo the thins of the Bodoni typeface."

J

The Consult's Favorite
Bodoni Letter is "J".

"A typeface with an established and crafted feel that was perfect for the project."

Worth Their Weight
2008 – Direct Mail
Client Skillfast-UK
Design The Consult (Alex Atkinson, John-Paul Warner)

Direct mail piece for awards scheme created as part of the Behind the Seams campaign. It encouraged employers to nominate "Skills Heroes" – technically skilled workers without whom their business could not function. Using gold foil 'seams' to portray a prestigious feel for the awards, the piece helped to generate national and regional press coverage and culminated in an award ceremony at the opening of the Behind the Seams exhibition in Covent Garden.

Typeface in Use
Bodoni Be Bold

Les canaux de la mode
2008 – Poster, Invitation, Exhibition Catalog
Client Orang'frog
Design Mainstudio (Edwin van Gelder)
Photography Barrie Hullegie

Les Canaux de la Mode is a collaboration between Dutch fashion designers and French craftsmen. The two-week exhibition kicked off with vernissages in both Amsterdam and Paris. The invitation for the vernissages came in a paper type that feels smooth on one side and rough on the other. The double-edged character of the project (Dutch versus French, design versus craftsmanship) is also expressed in the typography; a variation of solid, full letters and hollow, graceful ones.

Mainstudio's Favorite
Bodoni Character is
"&".

Photography hannahlipowsky.com
Location lafransa.com

bambi/

bambi/mint

bambi/bylaura

Naming - Designer Laura Figueras has used the name "Bambi By Laura" for some time. Laura gained recognition after various runway shows, as well as media and publication attention from the fashion press. However, the "Bambi by Laura" brand never managed to establish itself. Brand establishment met with difficulties in meeting the evolving business model from individual designer to company. It was a strategic decision to use "bambi" as an integral part of all activities and to add "bylaura" or "mint" when needed. This gives the company flexibility and strengthens the overall brand identity.

Typeface in Use
TpMartini (in-house type-face based upon Bodoni)

bambi/bylaura
2009 – Corporate Identity
Client bambi/bylaura
Designer TwoPoints.Net

Bambi/byLaura is a fashion brand based in London and Barcelona. Lead designer Laura Figueras has shown her work on the runways of Paris, Milan, London, and Barcelona. Her designs are sold at Topshop in London and she has recently developed a signature line for Roxy.

TwoPoints.Net designed a flexible visual identity design based upon a corporate typeface and corporate elements with infinite configuration possibilities.

bambi/bylaura

TwoPoints.Net's
Favorite Bodoni Letter
is "ß".

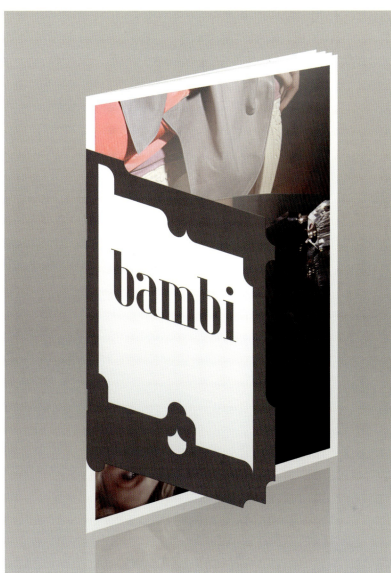

Look Book
"AW 09|10 - Narcissus"

Photography
hannahlipowsky.com
Location
lafransa.com

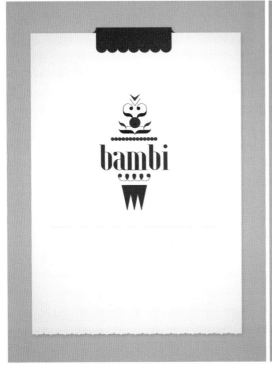

Typeface in Use
Bodoni, Trade Gothic

O

Ömse's Favorite
Bodoni Letter is "O".

Parklife
2010 – Event Identity and Collateral
Client Fuzzy
Design Ömse (James Kape and Briton Smith)
Paper Benja Harney
Collaborator vissukamma Ratsaphong

Our brief was to create branding materials for a music
festival that is on tour around Australia. These materials
would have to reflect the contemporary music at the festival
and highlight the beautiful parkland venues. To do this
we commissioned paper engineer Benja Harvey, to create a number of miniature park objects. These were then
arranged and photographed as the core visual identity
across all print, online, television advertising and event
collateral.

*"We decided to use
Bodoni as the pri-
mary typeface as it
supported the brands
position as a premium
event and worked
well with the elegant
paper engineering
and white space.
Trade Gothic was
used as a supporting
sans serif face in some
of the event collat-
eral."*

Russian painters and
travellers of the 19th
century
2009 – Poster
Client Museum of
Fine Arts Chaux-de-
Fonds, Switzerland
Design Onlab
(Thibaud Tissot)

Paintings and drawings of the Museum of History and Fine Arts of
Geneva exhibited in La Chaux-de-Fonds. The pieces, donated to the
museum of Geneva at the beginning of the 19th century, were created by writers, poets and painters on their road through Orient and
Occident. Poster Bodoni is used as a typeface. The title is designed in
Cyrillic and reveals a painting from the collection as graphic background.

Typeface in Use
Poster Bodoni

IN THE FLOWERS – 5:22

MY GIRLS – 5:41

ALSO FRIGHTENED – 5:14

SUMMERTIME CLOTHES – 4:30

DAILY ROUTINE – 5:46

BLUISH – 5:14

GUYS EYES – 4:31

TASTE – 3:53

LION IN A COMA – 4:12

NO MORE RUNNIN – 4:23

BROTHERSPORT – 5:59

Typeface in Use
Bodoni

"I wanted the clean, white, sleeve to contrast with the bright and colorfull illustrations in the CD sleeve. Bodoni provides this classy yet quirky feel to the whole package."

Fendy Ibrahim's Favorite Bodoni Character is "&".

Merriweather Post Pavillion
2010 – CD Packaging
Design Fendy Ibrahim

It was done for a brief for one of my illustration modules in NTU School of Art Design & Media.

"Elegant and luxurious"

3D Type
2010 – 3D Type
Design Make_Studio

Building on 3D type for our portfolio, we have taken a few
logos that we produced in order to show our clients a different dimension to type.

Typeface in Use
Bodoni

Make_Studio's
Favorite Bodoni Letter
is "O".

"The bold areas allows to re-shape the font."

<u>Typeface in Use</u>
Bodoni Std - Poster
(Adobe Systems)

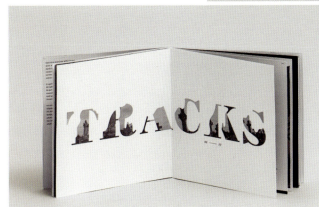

<u>Dancing with the dead</u>
2008 – Typography,
CD Packaging, Booklet
<u>Client</u> RISD
<u>Design</u> Janine Rewell

Typeface design and package
for an album that contains funeral music from different
cultures and tribes. In the re-shaping of Bodoni I was
inspired by dripping blood.

Epitalam - Festival International
de Poésie Contemporaine 2009
2009 – Poster, Program, Tickets
Client Epitalam - Festival International de Poésie Contemporaine
2009 - La Chaux-de-Fo nds,
Switzerland
Design idealismo (Chris Gautschi,
Laurent Allemann)

Communication development for
a contemporary poetry festival.
The concept is based on the idea
of the use of the video's symbolic
new media used in contemporary
poetry, as an illustration of each
support relative to its function. The
images are treated in black-white
to reinforce the contemporary side
and all the typefaces used are from
the Bodoni family in order to bring
up the poetry side.

Typeface in Use
Bodoni Poster,
Bodoni MT

Dodger blue is a shade of the color blue named for its use in the uniform of the Los Angeles Dodgers. It is also a web color used in the design of web pages [...] it is not the actual shade of blue worn by the Dodgers.

From Wikipedia, the free encyclopedia

Burly Wood

Submitted by David Kleijnjan "solid, sturdy, round, knotty, grotesque, squash you. this is an image of a Kauri tree, one of the worlds largest trees and takes 8 grown men to hug it."

"The project positions itself between man and machine, we felt that Bodoni having a long and romantic history was an interesting font to use in combination with Monaco."

http://en.wikipedia.org/wiki/Dodger_blue

Image right submitted by David Kleijnjan and found at: http://www.woodman.ws/Kauliby/WINTERS/NIKING/marchN3/Photos.htm
Image left found at: http://www.buliquout.com/villes/showdoys.htm
http://whitespoke.hexaplex.nl/burly-wood

There is nothing against having a central repository that links names to colours and then you could have millions of them if you wanted.

Hot Pink

So they are trying to direct it to the experience, but it is a pretty feeble excuse.
I did actually design something where you could combine key words, for example 'light', 'smoky', 'red' in a consistent way. I showed how it could be used and it gave you a reasonable set of colours that you could describe in English and know what you were getting. Because with something like PeachPuff you have no idea what you're getting. You would have to go and look it up. But like I said, that didn't get through because it didn't get enough support from the other members of the group.

Thinking about the tension between machine and man that this colour naming has, what do you think that the continuing use of these human language/color names such as WhiteSmoke can accomplish or even undermine when trying to set new and more semantic standards on the web?
Colour names are very culturally orientated.
I once wrote a long critique of the colour names because they are so culturally biased. The problem, and it's a big problem, is that there is no such thing as non culture biased colour names. All colour names are culturally biased and it is an interesting study in itself how colour is always interpreted in a culturally significant way.
For instance, Japanese has no separate names for green and blue. Traffic light is the same colour as the sky. I mean, they are two variants of the same colour, but they use the same word to represent the traffic light as they do the sky. It's an interesting study because you see how colours develop in cultures according to the environment. You can date the colour orange very closely to the year of it entering in Dutch and English to when the fruit was introduced in Northern Europe. Suddenly you had this thing and you were able to specify its colour. Up to that point the colour that we had that was orange was like a reddish yellow... and there was no separate word for it...

And the same applies to pink and violet. There are a number colours that you can specifically date to a particular point where we became aware of this colour as a separate thing.

The colour value RRRBBBB and its screen presence, just didn't exist in our vocabulary before becoming designers.
I have a lecture about colour, because there is just so much that is fascinating about colour. How we interpret it and how we see it. And how often we are fooled by what we see, because of the way our brains work. So it is one of the reasons why an HSV solution is better than using English words: there is no culture bias in it whatsoever. But on the other hand, because it is related to perception it is biased to people, whereas the current method is biased to computers.

The HTML Color Name palette consists of 140 colours, each having their own unique value such as PeachPuff. In an ideal world where computers and people live in harmony, how would you set about giving descriptive, maybe even semantic values to the 10.000+ colours that the hexadecimal palette can represent.
There is nothing against having a central repository that links names to colours and then you could have millions of them if you wanted.

Do you think people need those kinds of physical names for colours? Because that is sometimes the problem with the hexadecimal system.
Yes, because hexadecimal is just awful. It should be banned. If there is anything that should be deprecated it is hexadecimal. Because it has no relation to anything but the damn machines. And that is the last thing we need. The geeks who designed it in the first place, they don't understand these things, for them, machines are it.

Submitted by Krista van der Niet "Bed sheets in a hotel room in Paris."

Image top: Krista van der Niet.
Image bottom found at: http://www.glamguns.com/AK47.html
http://whitespoke.hexaplex.nl/hot-pink

White Smoke

Hexaplex's Favorite
Bodoni Letter is "O"

Typeface in Use
Bodoni,
Monaco

White Smoke
#f0f0f0
245, 245, 245
Submitted by Hexaplex

White Smoke
By Hexaplex

Light Pink
is darker
than Pink

White Smoke
2010 – Website, Booklet and Exhibition Graphics
Design Hexaplex (Micha Bakker, Cheryl Gallaway)

In the White Smoke project man and machine meet: the audience engages a world of color codes and names. On the eve of the information era, White Smoke lays down poetic and semantic tensions between man and machine! White Smoke encourages the audience to enter the information society with human, poetical effort.

The production for the publication and exhibition are in collaboration with the publisher "Onomatopee".

Design by Micha Bakker & Cheryl Gallaway © 2010
http://whitesmoke.hexaplex.nl
www.hexaplex.nl

9

café EAT ;	coffee & tea	
a gr-EAT	homemade gourmet	
tr-EAT		

cafe EAT
2009 – Corporate Identity,
Poster and Table Mat
Client cafe EAT
Design Workroom

This identity was created for a
small cafe that sells organic food
and coffee. Our task was simple:
how to differentiate from "EAT",
a British food company with the
same name.

Workroom's Favorite
Bodoni Letter is "r".

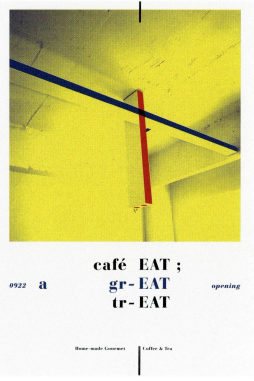

"In the end, we erased EAT (written in bold sans-serif type) using correction tape and then printed another typeface in a totally different style, Bauer Bodoni on top. This was possible due to the concrete structure which had the former signboard protruded from the wall of the building."

Teddy Bear Art Gallery
2008 – Identity, Signage
Client Teddy Bear Museum
Design Workroom

Typeface in Use
Customized Bauer
Bodoni

b1   TEDDY BEAR
            art gallery
            1

3f   gallery
            2

4f   i̇r   garden

2f   ▼r   cafe

1f   ▐▐   shop

"*Teddy Bear Art Gallery displays teddy bear artworks that are mainly parodies of famous paintings. We felt that the image of displayed bears is similar to that of Bodoni typeface with delicate horizontal strokes and round shapes. Also, we wanted the audience to experience something fantastic as a fictional character Giambattista Bodoni did in Umberto Eco's novel. To maximize delicate quality, we modified Bauer Bodoni, and also created symbols of a café, garden, and art shop with the modified typeface.*"

Dates
2009.
2. 17. Tue. –
3. 15. Sun.

홍대우체국

요금별납

Opening
Reception
2009.
2. 17. Tue. 6 PM.

Special
Workshop
First. Collection

본 전시는 2008 SITE
Santa Fe 비엔날레에
참여한 홍순명 작가가
비엔날레에서 발표했던
〈사이드 스케이프〉의
최근작을 소개합니다.

홍
순
명

SOUN HONG

Sazie m space
씨지 스페이스.

쌈지스페이스
121-190
서울시 마포구
창전동 5-129

SSamzie Space
121-190
5-129 changjeon-dong
Mapo-gu, Seoul, Korea

tel.3142-1693 / 4
ssamziespace@ssamziespace.com
www.ssamziespace.com

*"Simple. The artist pre-
ferred this typeface."*

Typeface in Use
Bauer Bodoni

Staatsoper unter
den Linden
1992-2002 – Posters
Client Staatsoper
Berlin
Design cyan, Berlin

Cyan's design for

The samples are taken
from a series of 56 posters
(8-10 per year).

Staatsoper unter den Linden was developed in response to
the baroque architecture of the opera building as devised
by Knobelsdorff in mid 18th century and rebuilt by modernist architect Richard Paulick in the mid 20th century.
In addition to the use of Bauer Bodoni typeface, gold as a
second colour alongside black recalls the splendour of the
baroque era. Images of composers or musicians as often
used in this sector of graphic work are abandoned in favor
of a strong rhythm of typography which fosters associations to music.

STAATSKAPELLE BERLIN

GENERALMUSIKDIREKTOR DANIEL BARENBOIM

27. / 28. Di / Mi 20.00   KONZERTHAUS BERLIN   V. SINFONIEKONZERT DER STAATSKAPELLE BERLIN

KURT DIRIGENT SANDERLING
SENNU VIOLONCELLO LAINE

DMITRI
SCHOSTAKOWITSCH
KONZERT FÜR VIOLONCELLO UND ORCHESTER N.1 ES-DUR OP.107

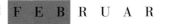

JOHANNES
BRAHMS
SINFONIE N.2 D-DUR OP.73

Hinweise zum Kartenverkauf: Theaterkasse der Staatsoper: Mo-Fr 10-18 Uhr / Sa, So + Feiertag 14-18 h sowie an allen bekannten Vorverkaufsstellen. Abendkasse: jeweils eine Stunde vor Konzertbeginn. Telefonische Kartenreservierung: 030-20 35 45 55 Mo-Sa 10-20 Uhr / So+Feiertag 14-20 Uhr. Fax: 030-20 35 44 83 E-Mail: comm@staatsoper-berlin.de Online: http://www.staatsoper-berlin.de Adresse: Staatsoper Unter den Linden Unter den Linden 7, 10117 Berlin

FEBRUAR 2001

STAATSKAPELLE BERLIN

GENERALMUSIKDIREKTOR DANIEL BARENBOIM

11. / 12. Mi / Do 20.00   KONZERTHAUS BERLIN   II. SINFONIEKONZERT DER STAATSKAPELLE BERLIN

SEBASTIAN WEIGLE DIRIGENT
ANN MURRAY SOLISTIN

HECTOR BERLIOZ——— LES NUITS D'ÉTÉ OP.7
ANTON BRUCKNER——— SINFONIE N°7 E-DUR

10. Di 20.00 LIEDERABEND
APOLLO-SAAL

HANNO MÜLLER-BRACHMANN BARITON
PHILIPPE JORDAN KLAVIER

WERKE VON SCHUBERT / BRAHMS

15. So 11.00 BRUNCHKONZERT I
APOLLO-SAAL
FRANZÖSISCHE MUSIK FÜR FLÖTE UND HARFE

CLAUDIA STEIN FLÖTE
NORA KOCH HARFE

WERKE VON MARAIS · BOCHSA · BOZZA
FAURÉ · DEBUSSY · FRANÇAIX

16. Mo 20.00 KAMMERKONZERT
APOLLO-SAAL
LIEDERMANN-ABEND

BERNHARD FORCK VIOLINE
EGBERT SCHIMMELPFENNIG VIOLONCELLO
HARALD WINKLER KONTRABASS

KLAUS HÄGER BARITON
KNUT ZIMMERMANN ORGEL
KATRIN SCHNEIDER FLÖTE
MATTHIAS WILKE CEMBALO
KINDERCHOR DER STAATSOPER

Hinweise zum Kartenverkauf: Theaterkasse der Staatsoper: Mo-Fr 10-18 Uhr / Sa, So + Feiertag 14-18 h sowie an allen bekannten Vorverkaufsstellen. Abendkasse: jeweils eine Stunde vor Konzertbeginn. Telefonische Kartenreservierung: 030-20 35 45 55 Mo-Sa 10-20 Uhr / So+Feiertag 14-20 Uhr. Fax: 030-20 35 44 83 E-Mail: comm@staatsoper-berlin.de Online: http://www.staatsoper-berlin.de Adresse: Staatsoper Unter den Linden Unter den Linden 7, 10117 Berlin

OKTOBER 2000

STAATSKAPELLE BERLIN

GENERALMUSIKDIREKTOR DANIEL BARENBOIM

13. / 14. Do/Fr 20.00 SCHAUSPIELHAUS IV. SINFONIEKONZERT DER STAATSKAPELLE BERLIN

DIRIGENT

FABIO LUISI

ANATOL UGORSKI KLAVIER

JOACHIM DALITZ ORGEL

JOHANNES BRAHMS KONZERT FÜR KLAVIER UND ORCHESTER NR.1 D-MOLL OP. 15
CAMILLE SAINT-SAENS SINFONIE NR.3 C-MOLL, OP. 78 ORGELSINFONIE

JANUAR Staatsoper Unter den Linden

STAATSKAPELLE BERLIN

GENERALMUSIKDIREKTOR DANIEL BARENBOIM

19. /20. Do/Fr 20.00 SCHAUSPIELHAUS VII. SINFONIEKONZERT DER STAATSKAPELLE BERLIN

DIRIGENT

SIMONE YOUNG

DMITRI SCHOSTAKOWITSCH ROBERT SCHUMANN
KONZERT NT 1 FÜR VIOLINE UND ORCHESTER A-MOLL OP.77 SINFONIE N° 2 C-DUR OP. 61

VIOLINE
MAXIM VENGEROV

MAI 1994

"Berlin's Staatsoper unter den Linden, one of Germany's most renowned traditional European opera houses, was one of cyan's first clients after German unification in 1991. Cyan won the commission for a new corporate design out of a limited competition. In united Berlin, the Staatsoper, situated in the east, suddenly had to face competition from the Deutsche Oper, built in the 1950s in the west. Main feature of the work for Staatsoper unter den Linden is the Bauer Bodoni typeface which is used in capital letters for text only posters. This design soon became significant for Staatsoper unter den Linden and attracted a lot of attention in the 1990s. For Berlin's Staatsoper unter den Linden cyan designed a logo, posters, opera books, a monthly maga-zine and various other publications."

S T A A T S K A P E L L E   B E R L I N

GENERALMUSIKDIREKTOR DANIEL BARENBOIM

10./11. Di/Mi 20.00 KONZERTHAUS BERLIN 1. SINFONIEKONZERT DER STAATSKAPELLE BERLIN

JUN MÄRKL — DIRIGENT
EBERHARD LORENZ — TENOR
TZIMON BARTO — KLAVIER

ANTONIN DVOŘÁK	SERENADE FÜR STREICHORCHESTER E-DUR OP. 22
MANFRED TROJAHN	SINFONIE NR. 4 FÜR TENOR UND GROSSES ORCHESTER (1992)
PETER I. TSCHAIKOWSKY	KONZERT FÜR KLAVIER UND ORCHESTER NR. 1 B-MOLL OP. 23

O K T O B E R   1 9 9 5

Parole #1: The Body of the Voice / Stimmkörper
Parole #2: Phonetic Skin / Phonetische Haut
2009, 2010 – Magazine, CD
<u>Client</u> Annette Stahmer (ed.); Salon Verlag, Cologne 2009
<u>Design</u> fliegende Teilchen (Annette Stahmer)

<u>Typeface in Use</u>
Bauer Bodoni Medium Italic (title);
Bauer Bodoni Regular,
Bauer Bodoni Italic (body);
Akzidenz Grotesk (cover text)

"The design of the cover refers to a red french exercise book (96 pages), in which I have written down the first ideas for the project."

Parole #1: The Body of the Voice / Stimm-körper« is the first in a series of publications dealing with the materiality of language and highlighting the theme from various perspectives.

This first issue is devoted to the voice and its "corporeality". This involves both the relationship of the voice to the body that forms it and which it leaves in the process of speaking, and the question of the extent to which the voice forms a body for itself or slips into a new body.

This publication is a collection of texts and works by international artists and scientists dealing with the "fleeting stuff" of language in an attempt to grasp it, make it visible and endow it with a body.

"Parole #1" is based on a design concept that works with the idea of a "body of text". Each article quotes in its design from the layout of an extant text which possesses an interesting connection to the relevant article, whether in form or content.

The textual bodies of the books are dissected, form and content are separated from one another and the old layout is "filled" with the new text. In this manner, the design of the publication contains 17 books.

Parole #2: The theme of the second issue is concerned with skin and its relation to language. The term "skin" is used here as a metaphor. It represents the surface, the protective sheath of not only the human but also of other "bodies" like the walls of a house, a product's packaging, the earth's surface, and so on.

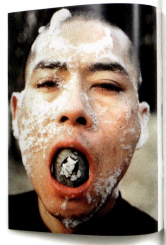

Skin describes the boundary between within and without, and is simultaneously a sensitive instrument for communication, directing external information inwards, and outwardly expressing inner states. "Phonetic Skin" is a poetic term serving as a starting point for a discussion of the connection between communication, language and skin.

18 international scientists and artists will present projects in "Phonetic Skin" which illuminate various aspects of this theme, including the voice as a vibrating phenomenon between within and without; drums; and works on architecture, walls, clothing, or skin.

fliegende Teilchen's Favorite Bodoni Letter is "ß"

Roanne Adam's
Favorite Bodoni
Letter is "f"

Bodkin Autumn/
Winter 2009
2009 – Invitation,
Lookbook
Client Bodkin
Design Roanne Adams,
Cynthia Ratsabouth
Photography Tina
Tyrell

Bodkin is a collection
designed by Eviana Hartman in accordance with the principles of
sustainability. The Bodkin Autumn/Winter '09 invitation influences
ranged from the designer's ideologies, the context of the presentation
as well as architect, Buckminster Fuller. The invitation arrived in the
form of a tetrahedron containing an airplant with care instructions.
One of Bodkin's green principals is to work within existing spaces and
with found materials. Therefore we held the fashion presentation at the
Horticultural Society of New York. The invite is printed locally with
100% post-consumer recycled paper and eco-friendly inks.

Typeface in Use
Bodoni FLF,
Trade Gothic LT
Condensed No.18

*"Bodkin as a brand
established Bodoni
FLF as the brand
typeface."*

The Vast Agency's
Favorite Bodoni
Letter is "g"

Alexander Boyd S/S 2011
2010 – Collateral
Client Alexander Boyd
Design The Vast Agency

Alexander Boyd is a family-run tailoring and shoe-making
business established in 1913. This A5 piece was used to
invite prospective buyers to a number of trade shows. It is
white foil blocked both sides on buckram embossed pale
grey Colorplan.

Typeface in Use
Bauer Bodoni BT Bold,
Bauer Bodoni BT Bold Italic,
Bauer Bodoni BT Roman,
Bauer Bodoni BT Italic,
Akzidenz Grotesk Bold

ALEXANDER BOYD mixes a re-
fine RED LABEL and heritage
LABEL. Both collections offer a mo
look with unstructured TAILORING
ties, scarves, knitwear and outerwe
can be worn casually and formally

"*The balance between masculinity
and subtly of the forms.*"

underbau's Favorite
Bodoni Letter is "a".

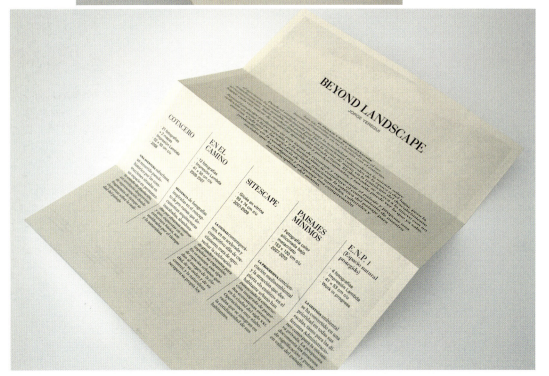

Beyond Landscape
2010 – Flyer
Client Programa
Iniciarte (Consejería
de Cultura. Junta de
Andalucía)
Design underbau
Photography Jorge
Yeregui

The presented flyer
was part of an exhibition by the artist Jorge Yeregui who
made a postmodern reflection on the landscape. The work
had to promote his thinking, so we decided to make a
reference about the nineteenth century English romantic
landscapes painters. We used a contemporary typography
(Bodoni), classic paper and used it with classic patterns.
The contrast between the postmodern work of Yeregui and
this romantic design enhances the reflection that the artist
presents in this exhibition.

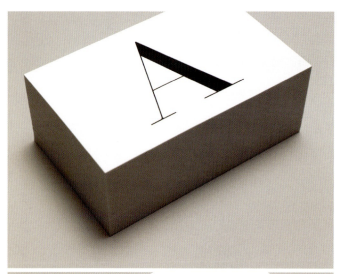

"We required an elegant, timeless typographic style."

A

Nelson Associates's Favorite Bodoni Letter is "A".

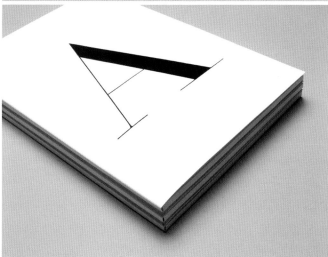

Anna McGregor
2010 – Corporate Identity
Client Anna McGregor
Design Nelson Associates
(Christian Nelson)

Renowned for her perfectly
judged weddings and parties,
Anna McGregor and her team
go to incredible lengths to create
exquisite experiences. With her
trademark creativity, imagina-
tion and unstinting attention to
the finest detail, it was clear that
Anna's brand identity demanded
something at once iconic and innovative. Inspired by the distinctive
aesthetic of Alexey Brodovitch's 1930's Harper's Bazaar
art direction, Nelson Associates elevated Anna's initial
A to her identifying mark. Whether stamped, etched or
embossed, the elegance of a consistent black and white
expression offered the perfect platform for her vibrant
event photography.

Typeface in Use
Bauer Bodoni

Anagrama's Favorite
Bodoni Character is
"&".

*"We applied a rigorous research
evaluating perception, visual
potential and aesthetics to deliver
a solution who responds both
graphic and functional purposes
to the field its applied and chose
Bodoni."*

Typeface in Use
Bodoni Bold,
Pistilli Roman,
Berthold Akzidenz Grotesk Condensed

B&R Abogados
2009 – Corporate Identity
Client Layers firm
Design Anagrama

We wanted to achieve a classic, timelessness, sophisticated look, with a touch of the yuppie lifestyle of the 80's. Creating an entity with a strong value a of trust, status and respect. In terms of design a custom typographic solution between Bodoni and Pistilli gestures, and creating a new ampersand with the DNA of both typefaces.

We Recommend's
Favorite Bodoni Letter
is "S".

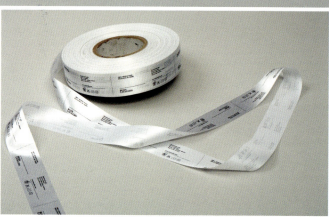

Visual identity for Via Snella
2008-2010 – Visual Identity
Client Via Snella
Design We Recommend
(Martin Fredricson, Nikolaj Knop)

Classic modern – Via Snella is one
of the new brands in the promi-
nent Swedish fashion industry.
"By combining the strength of
timelessness and the enjoyment
of the unexpected, Via Snella has
created male fashion since 2006.
We believe that the classic will
always connect with the modern",
says designer Lina Zedig. With an
ambition of international distribu-
tion through a strong brand, Via
Snella needed a visual identity
that could express its foundation,
and at the same time be able to
adapt to the looks of the changing

seasons within the fashion industry. We met these demands by creating an identity with one foot in
classic timelessness and the other
in the constantly shifting expressions of modern fashion.

*"Bauer Bodoni was chosen as type-
face to express the classic timelessness of the brand. And plays the
role as the most dominant element
in the identity. The identity makes
it possible for the brand to develop
over time and, from season to
season, change expressions while
resting securely on a solid base."*

Concert Posters by:

P.A.M. • ill–Studio • Stefan Marx • Josh Petherick
Alter • //DIY • Smal and Paze • Artus De Lavilléon
Museum Studio • Steven Harrington • Ryan Waller
SO–ME • French • La Boca • Sanghon Kim
Andreas och Fredrika • Filip Tydén • I:2:3

Curated by Thomas Subreville and Anders Jandér
www.ill-studio.com
www.museumstudio.se

Typeface in Use
Bodoni Classic,
Bodoni Roman

8

Museum Studio's
Favorite Bodoni
Number is "8".

Art of Music
2009 – Poster,
Invitation
Client Colette
Design Museum
Studio

"It was the best match with the concept and the headline custom typography."

Invitation for a gallery art show in the form of a poster. The Art of Music exhibition was 18 graphic designers silk-screened concert poster of the concert of their dreams. By altering music's own visual language; notes, a typographic music sheet in the form of a poster was created. The invitation has the same size as the posters in the show, 70 x 100cm.

"Playing with the thicks and thins."

HIGH LITE & LOW DOWN

Bic & Staedtler
2010 – Typography
Client Friends of Type - Experimental Typographic Blog
Design Ed Nacional

With my mind constantly on both letterpress and typography I love to think of ways to make type in multiple overlapping layers that work together. Inspired by Bodoni and making more extreme thicks and thins. I was originally drawn by a bright yellow highlighter for the thick highlighter and a very sharp pencil for the thin strokes. It made for fun experiments with thicks and thins.

Ed Nacional's
Favorite Bodoni Character is "&".

Typeface in Use
Customized Bodoni LT Bold

Neue Mode Initials
2005 – Editorial Design
Client Neue Mode magazine
Design Oliver Daxenbichler

Custom typeface design for Neue Mode magazine. "Initials" is a decorative typeface including only uppercase characters. The typeface is based on Bodoni LT Bold and combines the extreme contrast between thick and thin strokes with an overall geometric construction.

What Is Modern?
2010 – Identity,
Exhibition Graphics
Client Denver Art
Museum (DAM)
Design Cypher13
Photography Jamie
Kripke

Identity The concept of
modernism is typically
defined as or associ-
ated with the most cur-
rent, forward thinking,
application of thought
and practice. In creat-
ing the identity for the
Denver Art Museum's
exhibition, entitled
"What Is Modern?" we
attempted to decon-
struct the very idea of
modernism and in so
doing aimed to create something current, forward, new and representative of the immedi-
ate state of our graphic design practice.

To do so we chose to study the series of serif
typefaces commonly known as Bodoni and
classified as diode modern. These typefaces
were originally designed by Giovanni Battista
(Giambattista) Bodoni in 1798. In their early
stages of development they were considered
"transitional" typefaces in the field of typeface
design but as the Bodoni faces were refined
they later became recognized as "modern."
The "What Is Modern?" logotype is a function
of a detailed study into the refined simplifica-
tion of thirteen characters of one of the original Bodoni faces in an effort to produce new,
modern typography derived from something
epitomizing modernism over 200 years ago.

Exhibition Graphics To assist curator Darrin
Alfred, and the Denver Art Museum in com-

municating the think-
ing behind the works
in "What is Modern?"
and the exhibition
itself, title, text, and
label graphics were
designed.

The exhibition
graphics system was
designed to support
the works on display
and compliment both
their modernist aes-
thetics and functional
qualities.

"The term modern
in its simplest form
implies the up-to-date,
a current develop-
ment, or, better still, a
spirit in step with its
own time. Modern can refer to an 80-year-old
innovation that is still in use today as well as
a forward-thinking contemporary design. The
date when something was made is not as relevant as how and why it was created. Drawn
primarily from the museum's collection, this
exhibition offers a glimpse into the diverse
methods and ideologies explored by designers
as they respond to the compelling issues of
their own time.

"During the 1800s designers took advantage
of recently developed machine-based production techniques and newly available materials
to create unprecedented forms that added
diversity and fresh interest to the decorative
arts of their time. In every era since, forward-
thinking individuals, often in collaboration
with innovative manufacturers, have continued to demonstrate how an authentic search
for form can be both topical and intensely
personal. Ranging from the utilization of

THE QUICK BROWN FOX JUMPS OVER THE LAZY DOG

Typeface in Use
Bodoni Poster Modern

! " # $ % & '
( ) * + , - . /
0 1 2 3 4 5 6 7
8 9 : ; < = > ?
@ A B C D E F G
H I J K L M N O
P Q R S T U V W
X Y Z [\ ] ^ _

G

Cypher13's Favorite
Bodoni Letter is "G".

"Bodoni was chosen for it's timeless elegance and natural affinity to live alongside and simultaneously narrate all things modern."

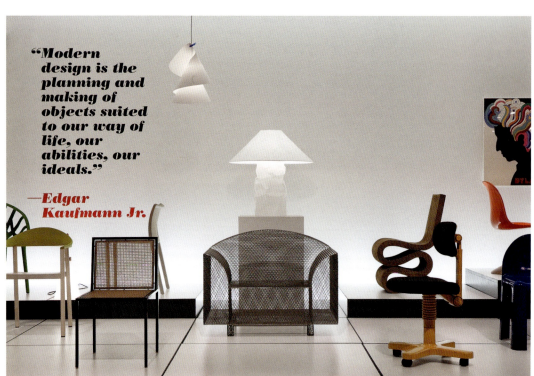

"Modern design is the planning and making of objects suited to our way of life, our abilities, our ideals."

—Edgar Kaufmann Jr.

large-scale factory production and industrial materials to the preservation of the longstanding craft values and traditions, as well as the development of a synthesis in between the two, design encompasses a variety of methods, materials, and concepts. And while these works may be of different generations, together they represent the past, present, and future of what is modern."

– Darrin Alfred
Curator, Denver Art Musuem
Department of Architecture,
Design & Graphics

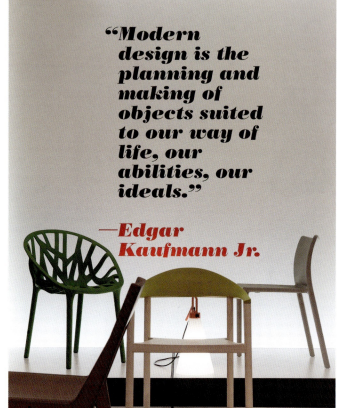

"Modern design is the planning and making of objects suited to our way of life, our abilities, our ideals."

—Edgar Kaufmann Jr.

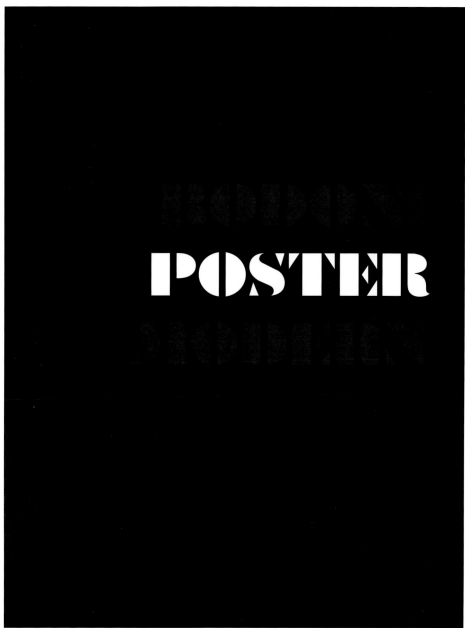

Bodoni Poster Modern Poster
2010 – Poster
<u>Design</u> Cypher13

We produce limited edition letterpress posters employing all of our typefaces. It was Bodoni Poster Modern's turn. This typeface was inspired and designed specifically for display purposes - there's none better than the design and production of a self-motivated, letterpress poster.

<u>Typeface in Use</u>
Bodoni Poster Modern

Typeface in Use
Customized Bodoni

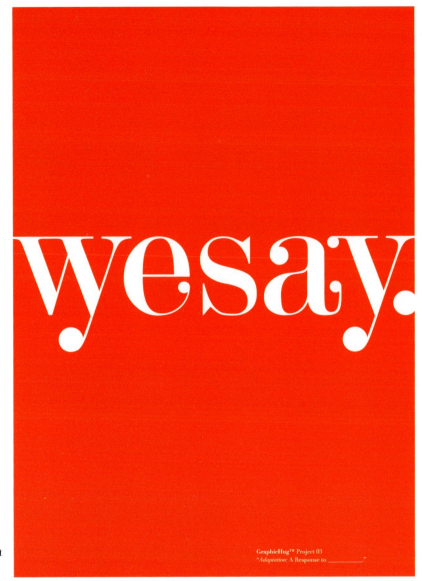

Adaptation:
A Response to

_____.

2009 – Poster
Client GraphicHug™
Design Graeme
Stephenson

Entering 2009 the
word change had
tremendous weight
on many levels. We
found ourselves at a
turning point with a
new president (at least
in the United States
anyway) bringing a
new saddle, a new horse and, hopefully, fewer guns to play
with. We were faced with an economy looming, as opposed
to pushing us forward, and a sense of urgency in regards
to the environment. Unlike years past the need, desire, and
momentum of change is greater than ever. These palpable
changes served as an appropriate theme for the very first
GraphicHug™ publication. As designers, how do we adapt
and respond? How do we communicate it? Are we instiga-
tors for change?

New Order
29 mei – 3 juli 2010

MY OPTIMI*m* WEA*rs* HE*lvy* B*o*oots *and is loud*

Corrosia! Expo
www.corrosia.nl

Typeface in Use
Bauer Bodoni Roman,
Bauer Bodoni Italic,
Adobe Caslon Pro

New Order
2010 – Poster
Client Corrosia, Alm-
ere, the Netherlands
Design Merz (Bram
Nijssen)

Poster for New Order.
The next generation
graphic designers,
curated by graphic
designer Herman van
Bostelen. The exhibi-
tion New Order shows
the work of a selection
of graphic designers
who have recently
finished their graphic
design studies at the
Utrecht School of the
Arts (NL) and have
been working on their
own practises for a
couple of years. The
works of these design-
ers all have a strong
personal nature. In this way the exhibition deals with the
question how designers find their balance between artistic
freedom and serving a client.

Bram Nijssen's
Favorite Bodoni Letter
is "W".

"Bodoni was used as a hom-
age to the LP cover of New
Order's "Substance", made
by UK graphic designer
Peter Saville and released
in 1987. After I took a quote
from Henry Rollins I juxta-
posed it to a completely different typeface. When you
do this, the Bodoni looks
even more like a Bodoni.

This way, the words are
visualized as iconic as the
aforementioned figures, or
at least I hope it does. While
any design looks like a
bold statement when made
in Bodoni, the typeface is
actually more subtle than it
appears to be at first sight."

DEHOTUN

Typeface in Use
Bodoni Ornaments,
Baskerville BT

"Dehotun has been born out of the demand for a bespoke and luxury service, which is a client focused, proactive property consultancy. Dehotun is resetting the standards within the Scottish residential property markets. We wanted to choose a typeface or two which mirrored these ideals."

Dehotun Branding
2009 – Branding, Stationery
Client Dehotun Properties
Design Kenny Allan, Pete Rossi

The solution was simple — To mirror the brands ethos and create an elegant brand that portrays a bespoke and client focused personal service.

19/11/08 — 21/11/08

GLASGOW FASHION ION WEEK

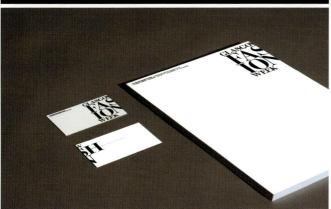

<u>Typeface in Use</u>
Bauer Bodoni

"Bodoni sums up the fashion world and the idea was to design something classical but set in a modern way to portray the progressive nature of the organisation."

<u>Glasgow Fashion Week Branding</u>
2008 – Branding, Stationery, Poster
<u>Client</u> Glasgow Fashion Week
<u>Design</u> Kenny Allan, Pete Rossi

Foremost elements of a complete rebrand for Glasgow Fashion week. The aim of the identity was to portray GFW as a luxury, unique and forward thinking organization within the fashion world.

A

Kenny Allan and Pete Rossi's Favorite Bodoni Letter is "A".

GLASGOW FASH ION WEEK

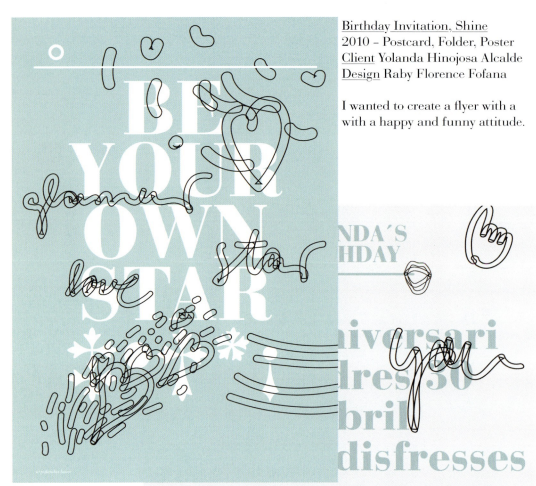

Birthday Invitation, Shine
2010 – Postcard, Folder, Poster
Client Yolanda Hinojosa Alcalde
Design Raby Florence Fofana

I wanted to create a flyer with a
with a happy and funny attitude.

Typeface in Use
Bodoni Extra Bold

Raby Florence Fofa-
na's Favorite Bodoni
Letter is "a".

"Bodoni is a friendly
and cute typeface."

> *"Bodoni Typeface is maybe one of the most elegant types ever. In this case, the high contrast and the vertical stress, results in a pure and finest composition. I could say that Bodoni makes us fell romantics."*

MISSING OWL
-
SLIM BLACK FEMALE
-
IF FOUND OR SEEN
-
CALL PLEASE
661 048 417

W

João Martins's Favorite Bodoni Letter is "W".

<u>Typeface in Use</u>
Bodoni Std Poster Italic,
Bodoni Std Poster Bold Italic

Missing Owl
2010 – Poster
<u>Design</u> João Martins
<u>Photography</u> Jim Ridley

Missing Owl is a sense of loss. Difficult to explain by words. Seni Özlüyorum LS.

R

Neo Neo's Favorite
Bodoni Letter is "R".

*"The classicism of the
Bodoni contrasts with
the contemporary
gradient background
and the geometrical
forms."*

Typeface in Use
Bodoni Bold

Clairbois - Fête de l'été
2009 – Poster
Client Foyer Clairbois Pinchat, Carouge
Design Neo Neo (Xavier Erni)

The poster represents the four elements (earth, water, air,
fire) with geometrical forms and colors. The triangle is
used as an esoteric symbol.

"We chose Bodoni because we needed a typeface that could cope with the high level of the symposium and brings up a totally different association than the word 'play' would do. The strong contrasts of the Bauer Bodoni are best visible in big sizes and create interesting holes through which one can see the picture of the background."

Spielformen des Selbst Subjektivität und Spiel zwischen Ethik und Ästhetik
2008 – Poster
Client International Doctoral Programme "InterArt" in cooperation with the Copenhagen Doctoral School in Cultural Studies, Literature, and the Arts

Typeface in Use
Poster Bodoni,
Bauer Bodoni Regular,
Bauer Bodoni Italic,
Bauer Bodoni Medium,
Bauer Bodoni Medium Italic

Design fliegende Teilchen (Annette Stahmer, André Heers)

The interdisciplinary symposium "Spielformen des Selbst. Subjektivität und Spiel zwischen Ethik und Ästhetik" (Forms of the Self. Subjectivity and play between ethics and aesthetics) at the ICI, cultural lab in Berlin, investigated whether and how "play" in its various forms – also, and especially, in light of its discussion in the context of post-modernism – could again contribute to a humanities and cultural studies-based discussion of subjectivity.

W

Bisdixit's Favorite
Bodoni Letter is "W".

Dalí 2004. Identity for Dalí Year
2004 – Identity
Client Fundació Gala-Salvador Dalí
Design Bisdixit (Pere Alvaro, Àlex Gifreu,
Carles Murillo)

Salvador Dalí is an icon in himself. The year
2004 marked the centenary of his birth and
the Dalí Foundation commissioned an image
to represent the different celebratory events. In
order to underline the personality of the artist, we decided to use his own image with just
minimum graphic intervention. A typographi-
cal bracket provided an elegant but convincing
substitute for Dalí's characteristic moustache.

ANY DALÍ 2004

ANY DALÍ 2004

*"Bodoni was Dali's
favourite typeface..."*

<u>Typeface</u> in Use
Bodoni

"*Bodoni Poster is a bold yet elegant font that has a commanding presence and an air of grandeur. With a brochure that was over 1 meter in length I needed to use a font that would not be over powered by the format of the piece.*"

Sam Frith's Favorite
Bodoni Letter is "X".

Sam Whiteman Brochure
2008 – Brochure
Client Sam Whiteman
Design Sam Frith

Sam Whiteman is a Sydney based artisan whose practice is dedicated
to creating exquisitely hand crafted furniture, artwork and interior

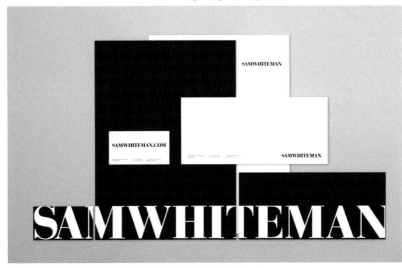

objects. Prized with the
task of promoting his
sublime work I decided
on a brochure format
that would match the
magnitude and impact
of the pieces contained
within it. The use of
the typeface Bodoni
helped to portray the
sense of opulence that
all Whiteman's piece's
transmit.

Blow's Favorite Bodoni
Letter is "c".

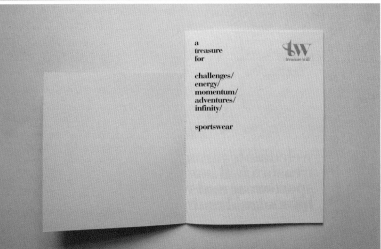

Typeface in Use
Bodoni, Helvetica

"The client would like to give a well-established feeling for their identity. Bodoni is well designed with a sense of classic."

Treasure Will
2008 – Corporate Identity
Client Treasure Will Limited
Design Blow

Established in 1986, Treasure Will is an apparel holding company that provides one-stop-shop services including sales, design and manufacturing facilities across South East Asia and North America. I was asked to design the new corporate identity, stationery and company brochure.

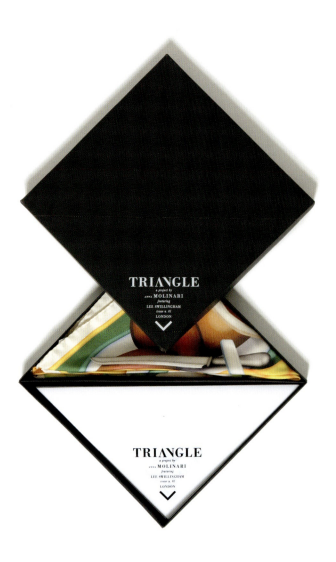

"Strong and elegant, good in combination with Anna Molinari current logo."

Typeface in Use
Bodoni BE Medium,
Bodoni BE Condensed Italic

Triangle a project by Anna Molinari
featuring Lee Swillingham
2009 – Project Image
Client Anna Molinari
Design Studio Blanco

Project art direction and logo design for "Triangle", the first scarf capsule collection project done by Anna Molinari in collaboration with English art director Lee Swillingham.

f

The Plant's Favorite
Bodoni Letter is "f".

*"With the restaurant
being Italian we felt
it appropriate to use
an Italian designed
typeface. Bodoni
Poster also has a very
friendly and confi-
dent feel to it which
suited the restaurant."*

Bianco Nero
2007 – Corporate Identity, Interior Graphics,
Exterior Signs, Menus, Promotional Material
Client Bianco Nero Restaurant
Art Direction The Plant (Matt Utber)
Design The Plant (Lisa Holst)

Typeface in Use
Bodoni Poster

This was a great project for The Plant to work on, along with the
bonus of fresh herbs in the studio used for making the illustrations we
enjoyed creating a sophisticated yet casual monochrome restaurant.

R

Helena Dietrich's
Favorite Bodoni Letter
is "R".

**MIR WAR PLÖTZLICH SCHWAR
Z VOR DEN AUGEN/ HIER DRIN
NEN IST ES JA SCHWARZ WIE D
IE NACHT/ ICH HABE RICHTI
G SCHWARZE NÄGEL/ DAS WAR
DER SCHWÄRZESTE TAG IN IH
REM LEBEN/ HIER SIND SCHW
ARZE MÄCHTE IM SPIEL/ SIE
HATTE EINST SCHÖNES SCHW
ARZES HAAR/ WARUM FÄHRT
ER IMMER WIEDER SCHWARZ/
ICH TRINKE DEN KAFFEE SCH
WARZ/ SO SCHWARZ WIE MEIN
E SEELE/ ER SIEHT SCHWARZ**

TIEFSCHWARZ

SOUVENIR / BERLIN

SANTÉ LIVE
SOUVENIR / REKIDS

06.02.2009

ROCKER 33

Tiefschwarz
2009 – Poster
Client Tiefschwarz
Design Helena Dietrich

My idea was to create
an atmosphere around the meaning of "black".
Therefore I used different sentences containing
the word black. Through the use of the Bodoni
typeface a dark and old/nostalgic style is created.

Typeface in Use
URW Bodoni Extra Bold
Extra Narrow

*"Bold and
strong effect."*

<u>Typeface in Use</u>
Sahara Bodoni

O Epicurista
2008 – Invitation
<u>Client</u> Loja do Banho
<u>Design</u> MusaWorkLab

Epicurista is a luxury store project that sells premium
products like perfumes, bath products, chocolates and
others. To make a premium invitation was the main idea,
presenting all the store brands and inviting to the opening
of the store.

*"Prestige and
distinct typeface."*

2

MusaWorkLab's
Favorite Bodoni
Number is "2".

Próject
Patterson

**Próject
Patterson**

Didda Hjartardóttir
Dodda Maggý
Elsa D. Gísladóttir
Erling Klingenberg
Finnur Arnar Arnarson
Gunnhildur Hauksdóttir
Hekla Dögg
Helgi Þórsson
Inga Þórey Jóhannsdóttir
Kolbeinn Hugi
Ólöf Helga Helgadóttir
Páll Thayer
Ráðhildur Ingadóttir
Sólveig Einarsdóttir
Auxpan
Apparat Organ Kvartett
ásamt Portsmouth Victoria
Synchronised Swimming Club
Hellvar
Ghostigital
Kira Kira

Sýningar
framundan
í Suðsuðvestur 2006

30. september – 22. október
Guðrún Hrönn Ragnarsdóttir

28. október – 19. nóvember
Hrafnkell Sigurðsson

25. nóvember – 22. desember
Gunnhildur Þórðardóttir

Typeface in Use
Bauer Bodoni

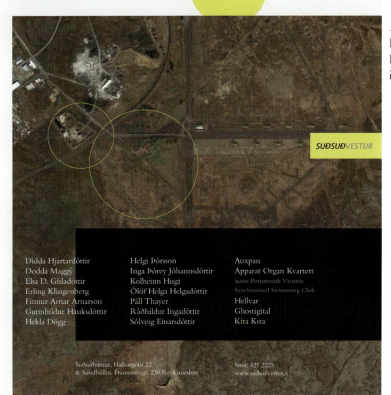

Próject Patterson

C

Ragnar Freyr's
Favorite Bodoni Letter
is "c".

Didda Hjartardóttir — Helgi Þórsson — Auxpan
Dodda Maggý — Inga Þórey Jóhannsdóttir — Apparat Organ Kvartett
Elsa D. Gísladóttir — Kolbeinn Hugi — ásamt Portsmouth Victoria
Erling Klingenberg — Ólöf Helga Helgadóttir — Synchronised Swimming Club
Finnur Arnar Arnarson — Páll Thayer — Hellvar
Gunnhildur Hauksdóttir — Ráðhildur Ingadóttir — Ghostigital
Hekla Dögg — Sólveig Einarsdóttir — Kira Kira

Suðsuðvestur, Hafnargötu 22
& Sundhöllin, Framnesvegi, 230 Reykjanesbær

Sími: 421 2225
www.sudsudvestur.is

Project Patterson
2006 – Poster, Flyer
Client SudSudVestur
Design Ragnar Freyr

An all-in-one poster/flyer/brochure/invitation
for gallery SudSudVestur.

TpMartini
2008 – Typeface
Design TwoPoints.Net
(Martin Lorenz)

Having been educated in type design at the Royal Academy of Fine Arts in The Hague, the Netherlands I learned that real type has to be drawn by hand, but to be honest I am too lazy for hand drawn type and too interested in grids and visual systems, so I was wondering if it wouldn't be interesting to use the traditional shape of hand drawn letters, but create it within the limitations of a 100% constructed type.

The typeface is based upon a square grid and three different basic forms. The basic forms consist of a straight line and two circles of different sizes. The line can be extended, but the circles retain their related proportions.

TpMartini

A1
Poster
composto con
il carattere
Tp Martini

© This font software is copyright protected. This font software and all copies are and remain mental property of the manufacturer.

Typeface designed by TwoPoints.Net
Via Laietana 37 / 4ª Planta / Despacho 32
08003 Barcelona / Spain

ABCDEFGHIJ
KLMNOPQRS
TUVWXYZ
abcdefghijklm
nopqstuvwxyz
1234567890
BODONI
SANS SERIF

CONTRAST
SANS SERIF
BEAUTY
SANS SERIF
ELEGANCE
SANS SERIF
BODONI
SANS SERIF

Typeface in Use
Bodoni Sans Serif
(customized typeface
based upon Bodoni LT
Roman)

FOR THE LAST

15 days

AUSTALIS

has been

wandering off

ON HIS OWN

EVERY DAY

AVSTALIS DIBVS XIII
VAGATVR SIB CO TIDIM
Inscription on a Roman tile
Museum of London, London

Bodoni Sans Serif
2010 – Typeface
Design Didem Ogmen

Bodoni Sans Serif is my attempt to create a sans serif version of the Bodoni typeface. The idea was to remove the
serifs from the letters and make them rounded while keep-
ing the essence of the original letters. The resulting typeface is characterised by its distinctive curves replacing the
original serifs and strong contrasts in the stroke weight.

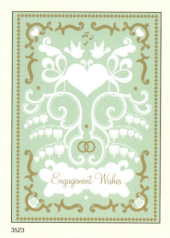

3523

3524

3525

3526

3527

3528

3529

3530

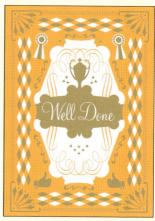

3531

Hanna Werning's Favorite Bodoni Letter is "W".

For You
2008 – Greeting Card Collection
Client Beaumonde Cards, UK
Design Spring Street Studio
(Hanna Werning)

"For You" – A voguish collection of 16 greeting cards for certain occasions for example Birthday, New Home or simply Thank You. Soft pastel colors mixed with decorative gold foil frames.

Typeface in Use
Poster Bodoni

"*The exhibition project was based around the idea that the design industry was over commercialised. Asked to create an identity for the exhibition we used the typeface Bauer Bodoni for its elaborate feel and this is something we wanted to communicate.*"

Shameless The Art of Self-Promotion
2008 – Exhibition Identity
Client Sassoon Gallery
Design Mortar&Pestle Studio

This project was an identity for a concept exhibition during the London Design Festival, where designers were not selling things they had made or printed but instead literally selling themselves. The idea for the exhibition came about as a reaction to the way the design industry was over commercialized.

We decided to design the posters and flyer invites as oversized price tags, which we asked the exhibitors to wear during the private view and a different take on the idea of selling oneself.

Mortar&Pestle's Favorite Bodoni Letter is "R".

Home
2011 – Poster
Client Nectar & Pulse
Design Anna Craemer

When your job is to travel all over
the world you want to have a cozy
homebase. Nectar & Pulse is a
fresh startup company not only
selling special travelguides but create a network of inspirational people, who want to explore the world.
This poster was made for their new
homebase in Munich to always be
reminded to feel at home even if
they are far away.

Typeface in Use
Eesti Text (by Tobias Rechsteiner),
Lydian BT Italic,
Bodoni Svty Two Book Italic

*"In this project Bodoni
was used because it
is the housefont of the
company."*

Anna Craemer's
Favorite Bodoni Letter
is "s".

"Bodoni expresses the Italian delightful way of living in every letter."

Inspiration
2010 – Postcard
Client CoachingAcademie
Design Anna Craemer

Many people do not want to become like their
mum or dad, and suddenly they realise that
they are exactly the same, with a very slight
difference. Doing the opposite of what you
do not like does not solve the problem. To get
out of the system and experience something
completely different, you have to take the risk
to step out that and find the synthesis. To live
the synthesis is always a fulfilling experience.
For the new year 2011 the CoachingAcademie
invites their clients to declare themselves to be
in inspired.

MOOD 08
2009 – Magazine
Client Mood magazine
Design Akatre

We created this typeface to make
the magazine look a bit out of
the norm. The mag represents
design, fashion and art and cre-
ates bounds between all of them.
We used a classical typeface as
Bodoni and redesigned the serifs
as an Elzevir. Also including an
"accident" (the little wave) makes
the typeface look contemporary.
The typeface, by the way, has
all the positive points a classical
typeface has. It is well drawn, the
curves are perfect, and it is associ-
ated with modernism.

Typeface in Use
Elephant (in-house
typeface based upon
Bodoni)

*"Mood magazine is a
melting pot of cultural
fields and artistic
fields. We used this
typeface because it
represents the mix
between classical and
contemporary."*

M

Akatre's Favorite Bodoni Letter is "M".

"Created shapes when distorted and overlayed."

E Roon Kang and Yeju
Choi's Favorite Bodoni
Letter is "2".

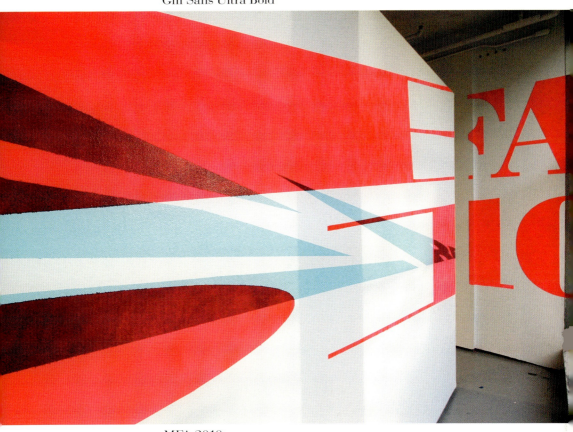

MFA 2010
2008 – Signage System
Client Yale School of Art, Green Hall Gallery
Design E Roon Kang, Yeju Choi

This project played up the basic purpose of gallery signage: to invite people into the space. While most signage is
designed to be seen head-on and from outside the gallery
space, this signage was distorted and illegible from that
vantage point. As viewers shifted perspective, they realized
there were two spots inside the gallery from which each
text appeared undistorted. Instead of presenting the information to a static viewer, this optical game encouraged
people to come into the gallery space and move around the
signage in pursuit of perceptual secrets.

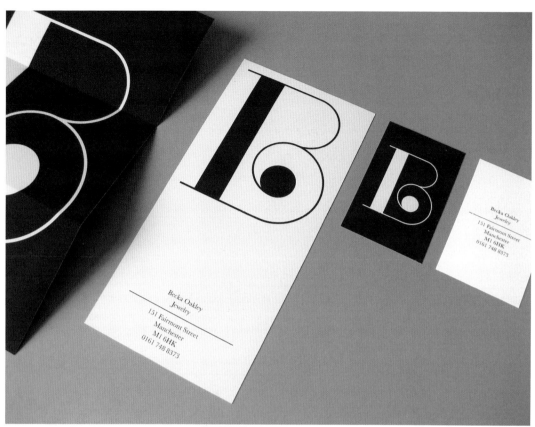

R

huvi's Favorite Bodoni
Letter is "R".

Logo was
inspired by
Bodoni

*"Elegant typeface
suited for jewelry
branding"*

Becka Oakley
2008 – Corporate Identity
Client Becka Oakley
Design huvi

Branding for Becka Oakley
Jewelry London

Becka Oakley
Jewelry

151 Fairmont Street
Manchester
M1 6HK
0161 748 8373

ILLUSTRATION
MIKKA GRO

TEA PAPER Nº 1

PAGE 20

SPOT
SING TEHUS

TEA PAPER Nº 1

PAGE 21

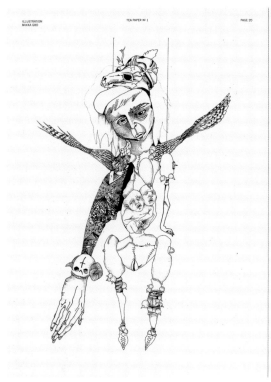

SING TEHUS

Allerede for 3 år siden kunne man dufte sig frem til Sing Tehus, hvis vision var at skabe et med mod formidlet at udbrede kendskabet til te af høj kvalitet samt kulturen herom. Te er ikke bare noget man drikker, men en livsstil for mennesker der forholder sig til det indtager og som beskikke en nysgerrighed efter kvalitative oplevelser. Der er en etableret et miljø, hvor mennesker mødes og arbejder erfaringer og inspirerer hinanden.

Derfor har det velrenommerede, London baserede magasin, Mono-

cle, også valgt at bidrage til Sing Tehus med et nyt grafisk design til en ny te-kollektion. Vi vil gerne benytte lejligheden til at sige tak til Richard Spencer Powell for det gennemførte og organiske design, som er blevet udvalgt til at slå på det nye danske designmuseum, Côte du design, i Saint Étienne. Samarbejdet mellem Sing Tehus og Tea paper er endnu et resultat af nysgerrighed og lysten til at samarbejde på tværs, hvor gode idéer opstår og endnu flere mennesker mødes,og giver en forsmag på hvad Tea Paper har at byde på og står for.

Teapaper No 1.
2010 – Magazine Design
Client Teapaper
Design Martin Ransby, Jonas Halfter

Teapaper is a Danish fashion and arts magazine which focuses on young upcoming designers and artists. As it was the first issue it was really important for us, in the design process, that we gave it a graphic identity and nice flow throughout the magazine. We did that by using only a couple of typefaces and few colors, which helped us to create a modern clean design that complemented the heavy photography based content very well.

R

"Its beauty and smoothness fits so well in Fashion context."

Martin Ransby
& Jonas Halfter's
Favorite Bodoni Letter
is "R".

Typeface in Use
Bodoni Book SSi Book

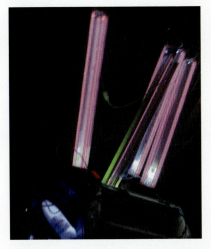

GLOWING TREE

Ti l器 optisk virkemiddel, generatorer og 10 UV kanoner får et træ til at lyse en omedag nat i Ørestadsparken. En lys idé, et strålende træ af København nye fælleskab, Tea Paper. Billedet rummer symboler på nyt liv og nye ideer, men også generationer det bure en metaforisk æstetik, der for drengene bag Tea Paper skal nå som en inspiration til andre.

Et projekt, der som bladet viser nye ideer, talenter, tanker og kreativitet. Tea Paper er en scene for unge københavnere, danskere, selvstændige og alle de ting de kan og vil. Om det er lysten til at skrive, lysten til at skabe smukke ting, lysten til at sprede kendskab til forunderlige ting, lysten til at vise talent, lysten til at inspirere.

Det hele sætter sig på vidt forskellige vis, denne gang i en kold park, hvor et tilfældigt træ sprøjtes med optisk opvaskemiddel, UV kanoner sættes til kroerfter hvor strømmer ud - det fanges endelig af en linse med billedtid på 30 sekunder. Et glum og den lyse idé er realiseret og fanget på ro og stemme tid, den given hermed videre og giver en formmag på hvad Tea Paper har at byde på og står for.

PHOTOGRAPHER: JASON IDRIS ALAMI
LIGHT DESIGN: MICHELLE JÄKKE BANNOW
TEXT: ISA MAJ LUDVIGSEN

18.15
-
07.02

Pisserenden

Enzo "Girls who are lovers, who like boys to be girls, who do boys like they're girls, who do girls like they're boys..."

Flora "Cheap beers, pool and pussy."

Bankist "Afterparty..."

The meat packing district

Jolene "Djuna Barnes, Trentemøller, Henrik Vibskov, Silas Adler, Mikael Simpson and a bunch of Icelandic people."

Bösendwerch "Fuck life"

Vesterbro

Ritz "Berlin Calling"

Festfodol "Nick... but still a bit fussy"

Nørrebro

Pråla Good coffee, nice furniture - buy it all

Sheit Shavarma Zieller pita kebab - 30dkr durum

Café N Vegetarian for a good price

Inner City

Zoo Bar "Zoo, oh how i miss you"

Bank Bar "Eggs beers and phones/ies"

La fontaine "Come on and jazz of with jazzy jeff"

Andex "We are the common people"

* Tea Office

Christianshavn

Månefiskeren Non alcholic place - you know it doesn't matter?

Duftlitet Little piece of history...

Christiania - Stalen "1. Go behind the bakery 2. Cokio and cake 3. I'm just a happy camper"

PHOTOGRAPHER: VICTOR NUNO

formdusche, büro für gestaltung
www.formdusche.de

Comprised of four graphic designers, Svenja von Döhlen, Steffen Wierer, Tim Finke, and Timo Hummel, formdusche is active in the broad field of communications design. Ever since its inception in 2004 formdusche's main vision, plain and simple, has been to conceive individual answers for each client's tasks. Both, listen to the client and form follows content, rank on top of their design philosophy charts. As their work is concept-driven, they like to irritate with typographic ideas or to find simple solutions for complex processes. formdusche's focus lies on corporate design, typography, book and editorial design, illustration, and communications strategies.
-pp. 30-31

Founded
www.wearefounded.com

We are a Newcastle based design studio, working across a wide range of sectors and media creating stand out brand imagery with effective returns. We are Founded.
-pp. 42-43

G Design Studio
www.georgiougavrilakis.com

G is an award winning design studio located in the old city centre of Athens. A busy, noisy, dark, multinational scenery. We always seek to promote an idea. To create based on each project's specific and unique needs as assigned by our clients. The whole process is quite complicated as the final outcome should always facilitate public dialogue. All projects launched from G clearly mirror us and follow the route of the idea behind them. Each project is a unique route, which we are always glad to follow. Simple and clear-cut forms reflect our ideas and characterize our studio. We design for the public view.
-pp. 32-35

Graeme Stephenson
www.thefutureinbold.com

Graeme Stephenson is UK-born graphic designer and art director currently living and working in the Middle East. He is also an active contributor and author for the design blog GraphicHug™
-p. 114

Hanna Werning, Spring Street Studio
www.byhanna.com

Hanna Werning established her own design studio 2004 in Stockholm working with self-initiated and commissioned work. Hanna has a strong fascination for patterns, whether it is the natural pattern of wood or something made-up and decorative. She was educated a graphic designer at St. Martins College in London and has since then been designing prints, wallpapers, porcelain etc. Hanna wants her work to be visually challenging but inviting, with an intuitive touch.
-pp. 140-141

Helena Dietrich
www.workwithhelena.com

Helena Dietrich (1981) was born in Munich. During her graphic design studies, she spent time in Stuttgart, Berlin and London, where she worked for renowned graphic designers. During her work as a graphic designer she found the time and energy to work on self-initiated networking projects in the cultural field and opens a small shop and gallery in Stuttgart called Salon VOW. On the way is the first issue of VOW magazine. Participations in various exhibition reveal her conceptual and reduced style of expression, related to her interest in typography and her associative way of translating everyday informations.
-p. 132

Hernán Paganini aka Puloverchito
www.puloverchito.com.ar

Graphic Design at the University of Buenos Aires where he taught in the art Morphology since 2003. He works for his studio Puloverchito for customers, both in the field of design and illustration. Hernán Paganini works as well as an artist.
-pp. 8-11

Hexaplex
www.hexaplex.nl

Hexaplex formed in 2007 to further and develop ideas on design that takes advantage of all opportunities in web communication. We see Internet as a network of connected web pages and sites. Without these connections the network can't exist. Ideas and dialogue within this network change constantly, creating a dynamic medium. We think content

and movement are determining factors for online design.
-pp. 82-83

huvi
www.huvidesign.com

Huvi, founded by Adam Robson and Matt Keers for a pure passion for design and everything visual. Our aim is to produce work that excites our clients and their customers through a playful yet practical approach to design that is tailored to their needs.
-pp. 152-153

idealismo
www.idealismo.ch

Idealismo is a structure created by Chris Gautschi and Laurent Allemann, graduated in Graphic Design at the School of Applied Arts, La Chaux-de-Fonds, Switzerland. Our work is a common point of view about our passion for Design and Typography. Our inspiration is reflected in editorial design, corporate identity and much more!
-pp. 80-81

Janine Rewell
www.janinerewell.com

Janine Rewell is a Helsinki-based illustrator and graphic designer. She has studied graphic design in University of Art and Design Helsinki (UIAH, Finland) and Rhode Island School of Design (RISD, United States). Janine won a bronze Design Lion at the Cannes Lions International Advertising Festival 2009 and recently nominated by Print Magazine as one of the twenty hottest new visual artists of 2010. In addition, she just had her first solo exhibition in Barcelona. Inspired by surrealist painters, children's books and toys, bright colors and the geometry of nature, Janine's designs are a distinctive mix of Scandinavian design and Slavic folk art.
-p. 79

João Martins
www.cargocollective.com/mpyd

I was born & raise in LVHC, Lisbon, Portugal. Now, I live in Barcelona, Spain, since 2008. The future, will be whatever we make of it.
-p. 119

Mainstudio
www.mainstudio.com

The Amsterdam-based graphic design agency "Mainstudio" was established by Edwin van Gelder in 2005. Edwin graduated in Graphic Design at the HKU, Utrecht School of the Arts. In 2009 his work won the Golden Cube of the Art Directors club NY 2009, for editorial design. Mainstudio loves typography, magazines, identities, illustrations and books. The approach is a clear idea or form solution, always playing with the context of the information and looking for something unique in every assignment. Main designing areas are music, theatre, fashion and art. Mainstudio works together with photographers, illustrators, art directors and motion designers. The agency is a member of the BNO, Association of Dutch Designers.
-pp. 62-63

Make Studio
www.makestudio.co.uk

We consist of a core of designers, directors, artists and creative thinkers with strong external links with our printers and photographers to provide an integrated network of interesting people. Using specialists within their field, we have also been able to adapt to needs of our clients and create a greater capacity for work whilst retaining overall project direction under the roof of Make_Studio.
-p. 78

Manifiesto Futura
www.manifiestofutura.com

Manifiesto Futura, an Independent Studio formed by Vicky González and Ivan Garcia aka Boronas. We love our work. We take responsibility of the results, because we're the ones who take care of every detail in our projects. We cherish experimentation, the value of the message sent & the intelligent provocation. We believe in function over form, celebrate clear content. We're Mexican.
-pp. 40-41

Manuela Dechamps Otamendi
www.otamendi.eu

Manuela Dechamps Otamendi works as an independent graphic designer, combining commissioned work with self-initiated projects. After co-founding SalutPublic in 2002, she is now

Roanne Adams
www.roanneadams.com

Roanne Adams is a multi-disciplinary design studio devoted to holistic branding that serves a range of fashion, art, and lifestyle clients. Led by award-winning Creative Director Roanne Adams, the studio offers design, image, and branding capabilities across a variety of mediums, from print to moving image. By thoughtfully distilling a client's inspirations, ideas, and motivations, Roanne Adams generates fresh, sincere, compelling brand messages that engage and resonate.
-pp. 94-95

Rob Schellenberg, Derek Hunt
www.robschellenberg.com
www.derekjhunt.com

Derek Hunt and Rob Schellenberg both graduated from Iowa State University in 2009 with a BFA in Graphic Design. Shortly after graduation Derek moved to New York City where he currently lives and works. Rob currently lives and works in Chicago.
-pp. 18-19

Romualdo Faura
www.romualdofaura.com

Romualdo Faura was born in Murcia (Spain). He studied Fine Arts at the Universidad Politécnica de Valencia (Spain) and has been teaching graphic design at various universities and design school in Mexico, Guatemala and Spain. Currently, he works as a freelancer, doing projects for his clients as well as for other design studios in Spain. He is specialized in corporate identity and Ethics in design, and a founding member of the association Solidus, an association dedicated to do design work to Nonprofit associations and NGOs.
-pp. 50-51

Sam Frith
www.samfrith.com

Born in Sheffield, UK, Sam Frith is a freelance graphic designer who has worked at some of Sydney's leading design agencies. He adopts a bold, typographic approach, whilst ideas, intelligence and wit form the rationale for all of his projects.
-pp. 124-125

Stiletto nyc
www.stilettonyc.com

Stiletto nyc is a design studio based in New York & Milan, that specializes in art direction & design for print and video. It was co-founded in 2000 by Stefanie Barth and Julie Hirschfeld. The studio has been featured in various international publications including Area 2 -The international guide to contemporary graphics by Phaidon Press and Grafik magazine in London.
-pp. 26-29

Studio Blanco
www.studioblanco.it

Blanco is an art direction studio based in Reggio Emilia, Italy. Headed by creative directors Sara & Valerio Tamagnini, Blanco has provided graphic design, web, event direction alongside image consultation since 2004. Blanco has also promoted several self initiated projects and events with various well known worldwide artists.
-pp. 47, 58, 128-129

Studio Ten and a Half
www.tenandahalf.net

Studio Ten and a Half is an independent graphic design consultancy, based in London, dedicated to producing unique and effective design solutions. Our work includes brand identities, editorial design, exhibitions, corporate literature, signage, packaging and websites.
-p. 59

The Consult
www.theconsult.com

We believe in delivering a quality service, in being direct, in transparent pricing and openness. We believe in thinking things through, in creative sparks, in ideas. We believe in building relationships, in trust and in honesty. We don't just believe this is what our clients want, we know it is, because we believe in listening. Our clients trust us because we have a proven track record of delivering success for some of the largest public and private organisations in the UK.
-pp. 60-61

The Plant
www.theplant.co.uk

The Plant began it's life in 2004, birthed by designer Matt Utber. With the help of some great clients and fantastically talented designers and project managers, The Plant has grown and now tackles projects across all sorts of media, spanning many continents including Europe, Australia and Asia. From our East London based studio we produce finely crafted work for a wide variety of clients in such diverse industries as publishing, hospitality, television, fashion and the arts. We believe in people and we believe in helping people so many of our clients can be found in the social enterprise sector.
-pp. 130-131

The Vast Agency
www.thevastagency.com

Vast is a design, branding and marketing consultancy started in 2003 with offices in Leeds and Nottingham. Our creative mission is to produce relevant ideas that engage, inspire and communicate our client's products and services.
-pp. 96-97

Tom Pollard, Ryan Van, Kesteren, Nick Dady, Stephen Ball, Paul Moffatt
www.tpollard.co.uk
www.ryanvankesteren.com
www.paulmoffatt.co.uk
www.stephenballdesign.com
www.nickdady.co.uk

Salmon magazine is a collaboration of final year graphic design students Stephen Ball, Nick Dady, Paul Moffatt, Tom Pollard and Ryan Van Kesteren, who studied at the Lincoln School of Art and Design, England.
-pp. 22-23

TwoPoints.Net
www.twopoints.net

TwoPoints.Net was founded in 2007 with the aim to do exceptional design work. Work that is tailored to the client's needs, work that excites the client's customers, work that hasn't been done before, work that does more than work.
-pp. 64-69, 136-137

underbau
www.underbau.com

Underbau is a project which came to life from the union, in 2008, of Juanjo Justicia and Joaquín Labayen, two freelance designers with years of experience in the field of publishing, corporate and advertising design. From the very beginning, the studio activity has been linked to art and culture, working in both national and international projects. Underbau's work is based on efficiency and design coherence, taking control of the whole creative process, from the initial concept to the final production.
-pp. 98-99

We Recommend
www.werecommend.dk

We Recommend is a multi-disciplinary design agency focusing on developing visual identity and profile creating design. We help companies, organizations and products to attract attention and be remembered.
-pp. 104-105

Why Not Smile
www.whynotsmile.com

Why Not Smile is an independent graphic design workshop based in New York City. Hoon Kim (Jeong-Hoon Kim) established the workshop in 2009 after completing an MFA in Graphic Design at the Rhode Island School of Design (RISD) in the States. Why Not Smile focuses on design for art, architecture and cultural clients across various media, printed matter, branding, exhibition design, motion graphics, and websites. Our current research attempts to visualize soundscapes in the public sphere to the printed space, in order to bridge the gap between the personal space and the public space.
-pp. 38-39

workroom
www.wkrm.kr

Located in Seoul, Korea, workroom is a graphic design studio and publishing house. In December 2006, a photographer, an editor and two graphic designers jointly opened the studio. Since then, workroom has primarily worked on community design and publishing as well as design services for clients. In addition, workroom helps run Gagarin, a secondhand bookstore opened in 2008 that specializes in art and design.
-pp. 84-87

First published and distributed by
viction:workshop ltd.

viction:ary™

Unit C, 7th Floor, Seabright Plaza,
9-23 Shell Street, North Point, Hong Kong
URL: www.victionary.com
Email: we@victionary.com

Designed & Edited by TwoPoints.Net
— The TwoPoints.Net team that worked on this book:
Martin Lorenz, Lupi Asensio, David Nagel, Kosmas Sidiropoulos, Raby-Florence Fofana, Felix Auer, Áxel Durana, Juan Ramos Pastor, Cornelia Brezing, Judith Will and Natalie Birkle.

Preface by Wolfgang Hartmann (Bauer Types)

Fonts in I Love Bodoni:
Bauer Bodoni D Regular
Bauer Bodoni D Regular Italic
Bauer Bodoni D Bold

Kindly supplied by Peter Rosenfeld of URW++ Design & Development GmbH

We would like to thank all the designers and companies who made significant contribution to the compilation of this book. Without them this project would not be able to accomplish. We would also like to thank all the producers for their invaluable assistance throughout this entire proposal. The successful completion also owes a great deal to many professionals in the creative industry who have given us precious insights and comments. We are also very grateful to many other people whose names did not appear on the credits but have made specific input and continuous support the whole time.